The Sharia Inquiry, Religious Practice and Muslim Family Law in Britain

In February 2018, the 'Independent Review on Sharia Law in England and Wales' was published, headed by Professor Mona Siddiqui. The review focused on whether sharia law is being misused or applied in a way that is incompatible with the domestic law in England and Wales, and, in particular, whether there were discriminatory practices against women who use sharia councils. It came about after years of concerns raised by academics, lawyers and women's activists.

This timely collection of essays from experts, scholars and legal practitioners provides a critique and evaluation of the Inquiry findings as a starting point for analysis and debate on current British Muslim family law practices in the matters of marriage and divorce. At the heart of the collection lie key questions of state action and legal reform of religious practices that may operate 'outside the sphere of law and legal relations' but also in conjunction with state law mechanisms and processes.

This cutting-edge book is a must read for those with an interest in Islamic law, family law, sociology of religion, human rights, multiculturalism, politics, anthropology of law and gender studies.

Samia Bano is Reader in Law, School of Law, SOAS, University of London, UK.

Islam in the World
Series Editors, Katherine Brown, Birmingham University, UK
Jorgen Nielsen, Birmingham University, UK

For more information and a full list of titles in the series, please visit:
https://www.routledge.com/Islam-in-the-World/book-series/ITWF

The Sharia Inquiry, Religious Practice and Muslim Family Law in Britain

Edited by
Samia Bano

Routledge
Taylor & Francis Group

LONDON AND NEW YORK

First published 2023
by Routledge
4 Park Square, Milton Park, Abingdon, Oxon OX14 4RN

and by Routledge
605 Third Avenue, New York, NY 10158

Routledge is an imprint of the Taylor & Francis Group, an informa business

British Library Cataloguing-in-Publication Data
A catalogue record for this book is available from the British Library

Library of Congress Cataloging-in-Publication Data
Names: Bano, Samia, editor.
Title: The Sharia inquiry, religious practice and Muslim family law in Britain / edited by Samia Bano.
Description: 1. | New York : Routledge, 2023. |
Series: Islam in the world focus ; vol. 4 | Includes bibliographical references and index. |
Identifiers: LCCN 2022050396 | ISBN 9780367547318 (hardback) | ISBN 9780367547431 (paperback) | ISBN 9781003090410 (ebook)
Subjects: LCSH: Conflict of laws—Domestic relations—Great Britain. | Domestic relations (Islamic law)—Great Britain. | Domestic relations—Great Britain.
Classification: LCC KD685.M3 S43 2023 | DDC 346/.167015—dc23/ eng/20230103
LC record available at https://lccn.loc.gov/2022050396

ISBN: 978-0-367-54731-8 (hbk)
ISBN: 978-0-367-54743-1 (pbk)
ISBN: 978-1-003-09041-0 (ebk)

DOI: 10.4324/9781003090410

Typeset in Sabon
by codeMantra

Contents

Contributors

Samia Bano is Reader in Family Law and Law, Multiculturalism and Rights, School of Law, SOAS, University of London. Samia has published widely in the field of Muslim Family Law in Britain, gender equality and human rights. Her forthcoming monograph entitled *Cultural Expertise, Islam and English Family Law* is due to be published shortly (Palgrave Macmillan).

Naheed Ghauri is a qualified family lawyer and an Associate Research Fellow, School of Law, Birkbeck College, University of London. Her research interests relate to domestic abuse, gender studies, religious arbitration and mediation and Shari'a Councils interacting with English family courts and human rights.

Elham Manea is a professor of political science, specialized on the MENA region and Women under Muslim Laws, a writer and a human rights advocate. She is Swiss Yemeni and works at the political science department, Zurich University.

Rebecca Probert is Professor of Law at the University of Exeter. Her research focuses on the law and history of marriage, bigamy, divorce and cohabitation, and she is the author of numerous articles and books. Her most recent monograph is *Tying the Knot: The Formation of Marriage 1836-2020* (2021) published by Cambridge University Press.

Islam Uddin completed his PhD in Law at Middlesex University. His research explored Muslim Family Law with a focus on marriage and divorce among the British Muslim population. He is an imam and a lecturer at a private institute in London. He teaches classical and contemporary Islamic law.

Introduction

Samia Bano

This edited collection draws upon original empirical and policy research to examine debates on religious practice and the experience of Muslim family law within British Muslim communities.

At its starting point, the collection frames the chapters around some of the key findings and recommendations found in the *Independent Review on Sharia Law in England and Wales* (2018) (hereto referred to as the Sharia Inquiry). The purpose of this is twofold. The first allows for a wider contextualization of the debates while drawing upon new research and engaging more broadly with some of the Inquiry's set of recommendations. The second considers the wider question posed by the Inquiry in relation to state responsibility and state protections as part of debates on multiculturalism, integration and legal pluralism in Britain: what, for example, is the role of the state and law in the recognition and/or accommodation of Muslim religious practice?

The book also addresses wider issues of legal regulation and the management of religious practices within minority communities and the ways in which English family law engages with and across cultural and religious difference(s). The image of Muslim family law as a strict parallel legal system, in opposition to English law and encapsulated as sharia courts, is presumed by many to lie at the heart of a British Muslim identity. The extensive media coverage on Islam and Muslims further feeds into a narrative that British Muslims are simply unable to fully integrate into British society.[1]

The focus and debates detailing the experience of Muslim family law in Britain have produced important scholarly and policy research, while addressing issues of 'women's choice and the use of religious bodies', questions of potential harm' and what constitutes as 'consent'.[2] The relationship therefore between the formal and informal spaces as inhabited by the state and the community epitomised by religious

DOI: 10.4324/9781003090410-1

bodies has led to important questions as to whether individuals from minority religious communities are expected to choose between two different sets of legal regimes for marriage and divorce, raising the potential for conflict between civil law and religious norms.

The Sharia Inquiry: Background and Context

The migration, settlement and integration of minority ethnic communities into western state democracies have led to fierce debates over the nature of public legal policies that aim to accommodate and recognize different forms of minority ethnic pluralism(s) and socio-legal practice.[3] One feature of this is the emergence of the 'multicultural family', one that is shaped by multiple cultural and legal frameworks, overlapping with the complexities of hybrid and contested identities based upon cultural, religious and ethnic affiliations. Liberal political philosophers have produced a large body of scholarship theorizing the relationship between identity, norms and normativity, rights, justice and state recognition and the relationship to human rights legal instruments and mechanisms.[4] More recently the focus has been on the potential detrimental consequences and effects of multiculturalism upon both majority and minority communities. The current popular discourse and narrative, therefore, is on the perceived failure of multiculturalism, leading to the emergence of segregated communities whereby communities live parallel lives. At the heart of these debates lies the question over the extent to which minority religious and cultural communities practice systems of religious family law with little if any legal validity, state recognition or state protection.

It was under this context in November 2016 the then Home Secretary Theresa May MP announced the Sharia Inquiry to be headed by Professor Mona Siddiqui. The focus of the Inquiry was to examine whether sharia law is being misused or applied in a way that is incompatible with the domestic law in England and Wales. More specifically, it raised questions on the potential discriminatory practices experienced by Muslim women as primary users of sharia councils. Examples of abuse, the experience of 'limping marriage,' Muslim divorce and legal regulation therefore lay at the heart of the Inquiry.

Prior to its investigation and the subsequent publication of the Inquiry report, it is important to note the tensions and divergence of objectives that became evident between women's rights groups. The announcement of the Inquiry led to some of the most forceful critiques from prominent feminist, religious and secular women's human rights groups. Several feminist and secular women's human rights groups openly criticized the Inquiry for the composition of the panel members, the lack of appointment of women's rights advocates and legal experts (with the expertise in national and international laws) and serious concerns over the impartiality and transparency of the Inquiry which led to some groups boycotting the Inquiry.

An open letter by Pragna Patel and Gita Sagal to the Home Secretary Theresa May MP opposing the terms of reference stated,

> By making these religious appointments, the government has lost a vital opportunity to examine the discriminatory nature of not only Sharia councils but all forms of religious arbitration fora including the Batei Din. Our fear is that in these circumstances, many vulnerable women simply will not want to give their testimony before theologians who legitimate and justify the very idea of Sharia laws on the grounds that it is integral to their 'Muslim identity'. Indeed, the panel is set up much like the Sharia 'courts' themselves.[5]

Opposition to the Inquiry therefore focused on the rise of sharia councils as a direct attack on access to justice for women and an erosion of their citizenship rights. Women's rights advocates however presented a complicated picture. The publication of the open letter prompted concern from Muslim women's groups that any opposition to the Inquiry would deny Muslim women the opportunity to draw upon their experience as primary users of sharia councils. The Muslim Women's Network organization therefore issued a counter letter. Shaista Gohir, Chair of Muslim Women's Network UK, stated,

> Muslim women are fed up of being used as political football and being treated like children. Everyone wants to listen to Muslim women when highlighting their terrible experiences. However, when it comes to the solutions everyone thinks they know what is best for them.

Further adding,

> Anyone advocating for the immediate shutting down of Shariah Councils are using women's rights as a guise to further their anti faith agendas and do not represent the best interests of Muslim women. Abolishing Shariah Councils would result in Muslim women being trapped in abusive marriages and drive divorce services underground, leading to even less transparency and more discrimination.[6]

While taking such differences into account, the diversity of women in cautioning against any recognition of religious tribunals was universal and raises important questions as to whether religious legal pluralism constrains or enables women's autonomy and creates gender-equitable outcomes. This is a theme that comes up in each of the chapters in this volume.

Report Findings and Recommendations

In February 2018, 'The Independent Review into the application of sharia law in England and Wales' was published.[7] Beyond the general and the more serious concerns regarding sharia councils within British Muslim communities, the past three decades have also produced rich ethnographic research including rich descriptions of modes of Muslim religious family law. One key and important insight is the limited role of state law in its regulation of religious norms and traditions including in the regulation of marriage and divorce. This finding raises the important question of *how* should the state regulate sharia councils in England and Wales? This question lay at the very heart of the Sharia Inquiry. For many proponents of the councils, multiculturalism and respecting cultural and religious in practice mean that privatized forms of family law dispute resolution should be left unregulated by the state as only a private regime of family dispute resolution can meet the needs of religious communities.[8] Others such as Southall Black Sisters and One Law for All argue that the state should be centrally involved in all religious family law regimes and abolish all forms of religious tribunals. The key objective of the report was therefore to investigate why sharia councils exist, their use and the reasons for their use.

The Inquiry findings included:

- Muslim women to be the primary users of sharia councils.
- The primary motivation for using a sharia council is to obtain a religious divorce.
- A significant number of Muslim couples fail to civilly register their religious marriages and therefore some Muslim women have no option of obtaining a civil divorce.
- Evidence of good and bad practice within sharia councils was found.
- Unanimous agreement among the sharia councils themselves that discriminatory practices occur in some instances within the councils.

- Sharia councils are fulfilling a need in some Muslim communities. There is a demand for religious divorce and this is currently being answered by the sharia councils.
- Those proposing a ban on sharia councils provide no counter proposal or any solution for anyone seeking a religious divorce.
- If sharia councils are banned and closed down this could lead to councils going 'underground', making it even harder to ensure good practice and the prospect of discriminatory practices and greater financial costs more likely and harder to detect. It could also result in women needing to travel overseas to obtain divorces, putting themselves at further risk. The closure of sharia councils is therefore not a viable option.

Further, the set of recommendations included changes to marriage laws, ways in which to encourage integration and to promote equality between religions in ways that should challenge misconceptions of a parallel legal system.

On the question of sharia councils operating as parallel systems and potential conflicts between civil law and religious norms including the question of competing allegiances the Inquiry found that,

> Common misconceptions around sharia councils often perpetuate owing to the use of incorrect terms such as referring to them as 'courts' rather than councils or to their members as 'judges'. These terms are used both in media articles but also on occasion by the sharia councils themselves. It is important to note that sharia councils are not courts and they should not refer to their members as judges. It is this misrepresentation of sharia councils as courts that leads to public misconceptions over the primacy of sharia over domestic law and concerns of a parallel legal system.[9]

The British Muslim identity therefore reveals important insights into the ways in which community formation and legal regulation and the rights of minority religious communities have taken shape over the past few decades. The chapters in this collection engage both broadly and more specifically with three key recommendations put forward by the Inquiry.

Recommendation 1: Legislative Change

The first key recommendation was amendments to be made to the Marriage Act 1949 and the Matrimonial Causes Act 1973. The changes are recommended to ensure that civil marriages are conducted before or at the same time as the Islamic marriage ceremony, bringing Islamic marriage in line with Christian and Jewish marriage in the eyes of the law.

It is interesting to note that the past few years have seen a marked interest in the nature and practice of Muslim marriages in the UK taking place within Muslim communities, with a large body of scholarship exploring the nature of transnational marriage, arranged marriage practices and strategies to combat the practice of forced marriage. This scholarship has also been accompanied by empirical research detailing the practice of Muslim family law in the UK and the emergence of religious councils such as sharia councils and religious tribunals such as the Muslim Arbitration Tribunal. The privileging of marriage raises important questions over the ways in which minority ethnic groups practice marriage and divorce, how different forms of marriage practices maybe accepted or recognized in English law today and what kind of change is taking place within South Asian Muslim families. Family law scholars have debated the formalities of marriage in English law and analysed over its form and function in ever diverse and multicultural contexts. Marriage today in England and Wales is regulated by the Marriage Act 1949 and the Marriage (Prohibited Degrees of Relationship) Act 1986 which provide for who can marry, where they can marry and at what time. In December 2015, the Law Commission produced a preliminary paper entitled *Getting Married. A Scoping Paper*[10] to consider whether the current law provides a fair and coherent legal framework for enabling people to marry, and to identify areas of the law that might benefit from reform. In 2019 the Law Commission began a review of the law and reform of weddings. In 2021, the Law Commission published its final report on the reform of weddings law.[11]

The linking of Islamic marriage to civil marriage ensures that a greater number of women will have the full protection afforded to them in family law and the right to a civil divorce, lessening the need to attend and simplifying the decision process of sharia councils. In her chapter, Rebecca Probert examines the question of reform within marriage that focuses on the laws of English marriage but one via a historical lens. She takes a 'long view of religious-only marriages', demonstrating that such marriages are not a modern phenomenon, nor one confined to any single religious group, but have recurred over time within different communities. The chapter shows that many of the earliest Muslim marriages in England and Wales were located within the legal framework, either by being combined with a legally binding ceremony, or, later, by being conducted in a registered mosque. It concludes by reflecting on how the same narratives and explanations have recurred in relation to different religious groups at different times.

Recommendation 2: Awareness Campaigns

The second key recommendation focused on promoting cultural change within Muslim communities so that communities acknowledge women's rights in civil law, especially in areas of marriage and divorce. This includes awareness campaigns, educational programmes and other similar measures to be put in place to educate and inform women of their rights and responsibilities, including the need to highlight the legal protection civilly registered marriages provide.

Alongside this, there was a strong emphasis on the need to ensure that sharia councils operate within the law and comply with best practice, non-discriminatory processes and existing regulatory structures. The Inquiry report states, 'In particular, a clear message must be sent that an arbitration that applies sharia law in respect of financial remedies and/or child arrangements would fall foul of the Arbitration Act and its underlying protection.'[12]

For many scholars, the question of personal autonomy and choice underpins debates on the recognition of religious councils and tribunals in Britain. The debates fall largely within two spectrums of scholarly work. The first can be described broadly as orientalist discourses which accord Muslim women little if any agency and personal choice as members of Muslim families and communities, and the second points to the fact that all debates on equality and free choice are circumscribed by questions of religious and cultural 'difference'. The extent to which free choice is therefore expressed can simply be one based on personal and strategic decision-making in the face of conflicting and competing demands.[13]

Thus, the language of choice, commitment and faith as described by the religious scholars fits in neatly with the discourse of belonging to a wider Muslim community (*Umma*) and the importance attached to the development and formation of a local Muslim community identity. So, what are the experiences of Muslim women using religious mechanisms of dispute resolution in matters of divorce? Do religious tribunals promote patriarchy and gender inequality?

In her chapter Elham Manea engages closely with the concept of legal pluralism as a contested subject of research. The presence of different groups of immigrants has raised the question of whether they should be treated differently according to their religious or original national laws. At the heart of the discourses taking place currently on legal pluralism lays the question of how to balance equality and difference. While her critique of the theoretical framing produces important insights into her original fieldwork, presenting the context and consequences of the application of Islamic Law in the UK Sharia Councils and Muslim Arbitration Councils engages closely with the Inquiry findings and limitations of its recommendations. Naheed Ghauri's chapter expressly questions the use of religious tribunals and women's experience of domestic abuse, oppression and inequality. While variations in the situations of women emerge, the focus on power imbalances and gender inequalities in mediation demonstrates a lack of safeguards and the presence of power imbalances between parties.

Recommendation 3: Regulation

The final key recommendation addressed in the volume is on the question of the regulation of religious tribunals. The history of sharia councils has now been widely documented in Britain[14] and can be traced to a diverse set of social, political and religious developments in civil society and as part of emergence of a Muslim identity both forged and as part of multicultural practices. The question of how such bodies should be classified and understood, for example, as groups, associations, institutions or alternative dispute resolution mechanisms, often rests upon the way they may operate and the nature of their relationship to multicultural practices and internal rules of process, institution, whether they rely on a hierarchal relationship and the structures and processes of decision-making and methods of enforcement. Sharia councils operate as unofficial legal bodies specializing in Muslim family law and providing advice and assistance to Muslim communities on these matters. They are neither unified nor represent a single school of thought but instead are made up of different bodies representing the different schools of thought in Islam. Many sharia councils are closely affiliated to mosques, and this reflects developments in Islamic religious practice in Britain. In essence, a sharia council has three key functions: issuing Muslim divorce certificates, reconciling and mediating between parties and producing expert opinion reports on matters of Muslim family law and custom to the Muslim community, solicitors and the courts.

The Inquiry further made clear the need to introduce steps to prevent discrimination and this could be achieved by the creation of a body that would set up the process for councils to regulate themselves,

That body would design a code of practice for sharia councils to accept and implement. There would, of course, be a one-off cost to the government of establishing this body but subsequently the system would be self-regulatory. This body would include both sharia council panel members and specialist family law legal expertise. It is to be noted that in speaking with the sharia councils, none were opposed to some form of regulation and some positively welcomed it.

In his chapter Islam Uddin draws upon original empirical research including in-depth interviews with British Muslim women, and interviews with professionals ranging from imams and sharia council judges to solicitors and counsellors and suggests reform and regulation of their processes and procedures to provide Muslim women with greater rights and protection.

Similarly, Samia Bano addresses the question of reform within sharia councils in her chapter and the potential for reform. This chapter draws upon the parity governance model to consider its usefulness while addressing issues of reform drawing upon the Inquiry critiques and recommendations.

This volume, in short, raises questions about the lived experience of sharia councils and Muslim legal pluralism in Britain and the role of the state and law in regulating Muslim marriage and divorce. It specifically draws upon some of the key findings and recommendations of the Sharia Inquiry and raises wider questions on the rights of minority religious communities, posing as many questions as it answers.

Notes

1 Salman Sayyid and AbdoolKarim Vakil (eds) (2009) *Thinking through Islamophobia: Global* Perspectives (London, Hurst Press 2009).
2 Samia Bano (2012) *Muslim Women and Shari'ah Councils: Transcending the Boundaries of Community and Law* (Palgrave MacMillan); John Bowen (2016) *On British Islam. Religion, Law and Everyday Practice in Sharia Councils* (Princeton University Press). Elham Manea (2016) *Women and Shari'a Law: The Impact of Legal Pluralism in the UK* (London, I.B. Tauris).
3 Tariq Modood (2019) *Essays on Secularism and Multiculturalism* (London, Bowmen and Littlefield).
4 Will Kymlicka (1996) *Multicultural Citizenship: A Liberal Theory of Minority Rights* (Oxford, Clarendon Press).
5 https://onelawforall.org.uk/open-letter-to-the-home-secretary/(last accessed 5th September 2022).

6 https://inews.co.uk/news/uk/open-letter-muslim-women-government-sharia-councils-28329 (last accessed 5th September 2022).
7 https://assets.publishing.service.gov.uk/government/uploads/system/uploads/attachment_data/file/678478/6.4152_HO_CPFG_Report_into_Sharia_Law_in_the_UK_WEB.pdf.
8 See A. Pearl and W. F. Menski (1998) *Muslim Family Law* (Oxford, Sweet and Maxwell).
9 Ibid p15.
10 https://www.lawcom.gov.uk/app/uploads/2015/12/Getting_Married_scoping_paper.pdf.
11 https://s3-eu-west-2.amazonaws.com/lawcom-prod-storage-11jsxou24uy7q/uploads/2022/07/A-new-weddings-law-LC-report.pdf.
12 Ibid n8 p14.
13 R. Grillo (2015) *Muslim Families, Politics and the Law, A Legal Industry in Multicultural Britai*n (London, Routledge).
14 S. Bano (2012a) *Shariah Councils and Muslim Women: Transcending the Boundaries of Community and Law* (Basingstoke, Palgrave Macmillan); R. Parveen (2017) Do Sharia Councils Meet the Needs of Muslim Women? In S. Bano (ed) *Gender and Justice in Family Law Disputes, Women, Mediation and Religious Arbitration* (London, Brandeis University Press).

1 Religious-Only Marriages in England and Wales

Taking the Long View

Rebecca Probert

Introduction

Religious-only marriages in England and Wales have attracted much attention in recent years. The focus of many campaigners,[1] almost all of the policy debates,[2] and much of the academic discussion[3] has been on the incidence of such marriages within Muslim communities. As Rehana Parveen has noted, '[t]he narrative around Muslim marriage practices has been to present them as uniquely challenging in this context'.[4] This focus has fostered an assumption that the law differentiates between Muslim marriages and those conducted according to the rites of other religions. This was encapsulated in the proposal of the *Independent review* that the law be reformed in order 'to ensure that civil marriages are conducted before or at the same time as the Islamic marriage ceremony, bringing Islamic marriage in line with Christian and Jewish marriage in the eyes of the law'.[5]

Yet the current legal framework already applies to Islamic marriage ceremonies in exactly the same way as it applies to all Christian denominations other than Anglicans and Quakers, and the differences between this framework and that applicable to Jewish marriages are not as great as is often assumed.[6] And history tells us that religious-only marriages have also occurred within Christian and Jewish communities. This chapter highlights a number of examples that have particular resonance for current debates. The first section focuses on the period immediately before and after the passage of the Marriage Act 1836 that forms the basis of the current law.[7] It highlights the debates surrounding Catholic religious-only marriages in the 1820s and 1830s, and how such religious-only marriages continued to take place even once Catholics were able to marry in a way that was legally recognized. The second section examines the emergence of Jewish religious-only marriages in the later part of the nineteenth century.

DOI: 10.4324/9781003090410-2

Much has been made of the special status of Jewish marriages, but, as this section shows, Jewish marriages nevertheless took place outside that legal framework.

By taking the long view, and looking at these earlier examples of religious-only marriages, we can see that exactly the same challenges have occurred before and that there is nothing intrinsically or uniquely challenging about Muslim marriage practices. The third and final section considers why Muslim marriages were not put on the same footing as Jewish (and Quaker) marriages. It also provides an insight into the first mosque weddings in England, towards the end of the nineteenth century, showing how those marrying there navigated the requirements of the law.

Catholic Religious-Only Marriages and the Making of the Marriage Act 1836

Under the Clandestine Marriages Act of 1753 and its replacement, the Marriage Act of 1823, the only route to a legally recognized ceremony was to marry after ecclesiastical preliminaries in an Anglican church.[8] An exception existed for the marriages of Quakers and Jews – and for members of the Royal family – although neither the 1753 Act nor its successor specified what was required for such marriages or what their status was.[9] Despite this insistence on an Anglican ceremony in the overwhelming majority of cases, the evidence suggests that religious-only marriages were rare during the second half of the eighteenth century. Such religious-only marriages as did occur were most likely to be Anglican ceremonies where the parties had failed to comply with some element of the legal framework.[10] The Quakers apart, Protestant dissenting denominations had not developed their own marriage practices before 1754 and so married in the Church of England without any additional ceremony.[11] English Catholics, by contrast, had navigated the competing requirements of conscience and law by having two ceremonies, either on the same day or with the Catholic ceremony preceding the Anglican one.[12]

It was only in the early nineteenth century, with increased immigration from Ireland, that religious-only marriages began to occur on any significant scale. Irish Catholic immigrants were thought to be far more likely than their English religious counterparts to be married by a Catholic priest without going through the legally required Anglican rite.[13] The result, those seeking reform claimed, was that these religious-only marriages were all too often repudiated at a later date, 'rendering the most sacred obligations subservient to the transitory indulgence of criminal passions', and bastardizing any children of the union.[14]

Throughout the parliamentary debates in the 1820s and 1830s over the non-recognition of Catholic marriages, comparisons were drawn between the law of England and that of the couple's country of origin. As one MP argued, '[i]n their own country they could be married by the Catholic priest, and the marriage was legal'.[15] The fact that Ireland was now part of the United Kingdom made this argument all the more compelling: one Catholic bishop, Dr William Poynter, pointed out that 'the conditions to which the Roman Catholics in England are subjected, in this respect, are not exacted from their fellow subjects of their own communion in Ireland, nor in Scotland'.[16]

Considerable emphasis was placed on the hardships to the wives and children resulting from the non-recognition of Catholic marriages conducted in England. Mr O'Connell alluded to the way in which

> a married woman, however respectable, and who had never done anything to violate the laws of society, might, at the end of eight or ten years, if her husband thought proper to select a younger or more pleasing partner, be left upon the parish with eight or ten children, the whole of whom would be bastardized.[17]

Those tasked with administering the poor law in the big London parish of St Luke drew attention to the fact that the children of these religious-only marriages derived no settlement from their parents but were chargeable to the parish where they had been born; the result was that they were a burden on the rates, and, 'unblest by relative protection, are exposed to pauperism, seduction, immorality, and every anti-social crime'. In their view, 'great moral evils, much individual calamity, and many public and parochial injuries, result from these circumstances'.[18]

As this suggests, the numbers involved were thought to be large. The parish authorities in St Luke referred to 'thousands of such marriages being annually celebrated' and warned that the resulting 'evils and injuries' were 'far more numerous … than persons not conversant with the subject apprehend or believe'. The MP who had introduced the bill emphasized its urgency because a 'dozen cases likely to cause bastardy occurred in a single day'.[19] And another put the overall number of Catholic marriages at over four times this, suggesting that '[u]pwards of twenty thousand Roman Catholic marriages would probably take place in the course of the year'.[20] Such figures were no doubt exaggerated, but in the absence of any reliable data they had an impact.

In terms of possible remedies, some suggested that the remedy lay within the community itself. Dr Lushington thought that the Catholic clergy could solve the problem by simply refusing 'to celebrate any marriage between Roman Catholics, unless they produced to him a certificate of the marriage having been legalized by the act of the Protestant clergyman'.[21] The problem with this proposal, as Mr O'Connell pointed out, was that Catholic clergy 'dared not oppose any impediment' to the marriage of a Catholic couple. At the other end of the spectrum, there were occasional suggestions that Catholics could be placed on the same footing as Jews and Quakers. These, however, were never seriously pursued. All of the bills that were considered by Parliament involved at least some formalities beyond those involved in the Catholic rite itself.[22] The challenge for reformers was to find a solution that would work not just for Catholics but for the far larger number of Protestant Dissenters who had no tradition of conducting their own marriages but who were similarly chafing under the necessity of marrying according to Anglican rites.[23]

While the incidence of Catholic religious-only marriages clearly played some part in encouraging a perception that reform was needed, Catholic marriage practices had relatively little impact on the terms of the measure that was eventually adopted. It was the Protestant Dissenters who dominated the debates, and it was the sheer diversity of ideologies and organization within Protestant dissent that shaped the terms of the Marriage Act 1836.

Proposals for sectarian reform having been abandoned, and several different proposals for reform having been advanced but proving unpopular, the 1836 Act was, inevitably, something of a compromise. It enabled Catholics and other Dissenters to marry in their own places of worship, but only once that place of worship had been registered. In addition, the marriage had to take place in the presence of a registrar, and after due notice had been given to the civil authorities.[24]

In practice, however, while Catholics were more likely than other groups to register their places of worship for marriage and to marry there once they were registered,[25] there were still instances of religious-only marriages prior to a legally recognized marriage in the Anglican church or in the office of the superintendent registrar. There were also concern among the authorities that such religious-only marriages were still taking place. In 1855 the General Register Office wrote to the Law Officers to seek their view of the status of marriages where there had been only partial engagement with the requirements of the 1836 Act. These included cases where Catholic couples who had been living 'in a state of concubinage' were persuaded to go through a private ceremony of marriage before the priest in a registered place of worship but without giving notice, and cases where the couple had given notice but then married before the priest in the absence of the registrar, and 'resting satisfied it is presumed (under the advice of the Priest) with the Catholic marriage thus performed they afterwards neglect the legal ceremony altogether'.[26] While it was recognized that such ceremonies were 'according to the law of the Roman Catholic Church ... considered valid & binding before God & the Church', the view of the Law Officers was that the marriages would be void. They also suggested that the priest would be guilty of a felony in such cases, as well as where a Catholic ceremony was performed before or after a legally binding one.

For present purposes, the significance of this exchange lies in how it illustrates the tension that existed between different conceptions of marriage. The Christian status of a marriage was clearly no guarantee of its legal recognition. Nor, indeed, was the fact that a particular religion was expressly mentioned in the Marriage Act, as the next section will show.

Jewish Religious-Only Marriages

Jewish communities were the only non-Christian group of any numerical significance in England and Wales in the eighteenth century, numbering around 8,000 in 1750, and between 20,000 and 26,000 by the 1780s.[27] The fact that Jewish marriages had been exempted from the need to comply with the requirements of the Clandestine Marriages Act 1753 formed the basis of later arguments in favour of the recognition of Jewish marriages.[28] After all, if Jews were not expected to get married in the Anglican church,[29] then to insist that the ecclesiastical courts only recognize marriages conducted in church would be to deny Jewish couples all remedies under matrimonial law.[30] As Sir William Wynne noted, the statutory exception constituted 'a strong recognition of the validity of such marriages'.[31]

The ecclesiastical courts had taken the view that the validity of a Jewish marriage had to be tested by reference to Jewish law.[32] The anomaly of an ecclesiastical court exercising jurisdiction over Jewish marriages was resolved by treating the issue as one of foreign law. In a number of cases, however, a failure to comply with Jewish law *had* resulted in a number of ceremonies not being recognized[33] – a point which underlines the fact that devolving regulation to religious authorities does not inevitably result in legal recognition.

The special treatment of Jewish marriages came under a certain degree of scrutiny in the debates over reform prior to 1836. Those seeking to be able to marry according to their own rites frequently asked why Jews – along with members of the Society of Friends – should alone be exempted from the necessity of marrying in the Anglican church. But rather than exemptions being extended to new groups, Jews and Quakers were brought within the scope of the new legislation.

The Marriage Act 1836 echoed the ambiguities of its predecessor in providing that Quakers and Jews could 'continue to contract and solemnise marriages' according to their own usages.[34] Unlike other non-Anglican religious groups, their places of worship did not have to be registered for marriage, no declarations or vows were prescribed, there was no specific legislative provision that witnesses had to be present,[35] and the presence of a registrar was not required. Instead, the legislation governing the registration of marriages devolved responsibility to Quaker and Jewish bodies to certify who would be responsible for registering them.[36] In the case of Jewish marriages, it was the London Committee of Deputies of British Jews, more usually referred to as the Board of Deputies.[37] At the same time, future marriages were declared to be valid only on condition that notice was given to the registrar and a certificate issued to authorize the marriage.[38]

This represented an important shift in the regulation of Jewish marriages. The fact that they now had to take place within a formal legal framework – albeit a permissive one – raised questions as to what the status of such marriages would be if they did not comply. The annulling provision set out in the Marriage Act 1836 had declared that if 'any persons' knowingly and wilfully married without complying with certain formalities, then the marriage would be void.[39] Unlike a number of other provisions, it made no explicit reference to Jewish (or Quaker) marriages, and not all of the failures listed were relevant to such marriages. Nonetheless, deficiencies such as marrying without giving notice, or in a place other than that specified in the notice, or without a certificate being duly issued could clearly apply to Jewish and Quaker marriages just as much as they did to marriages in registered buildings or in the office of the superintendent registrar.

In the first few decades following the Marriage Act 1836 there do not seem to have been any issues with Jewish marriages taking place outside the legal framework. When the Reformist West London

Synagogue established itself as a breakaway group in the 1840s and was denied recognition by the Board of Deputies, its members compromised by combining a marriage in the register office with a Jewish ceremony. It did not conduct its own legally recognized marriages until it was able to register itself as a place of worship.[40]

Again, it was increasing immigration that led to a change in practice. At mid-century the Jewish population was estimated to number 30,000 to 35,000; by the end of the 1870s it had reached over 60,000, and it was to more than double by the end of the century.[41] With increasing numbers of migrants from Poland and Russia arriving in England it was unsurprising that many were believed to be marrying in the form that was familiar to them rather than ascertaining what was required for a marriage under English law. Reports of Jewish weddings being performed by foreign rabbis with no authority to register the marriage began to appear from the late 1860s[42] and increased during the 1870s.[43] It was suggested that such religious-only marriages were facilitated by the simplicity of the Jewish marriage ceremony and by the lack of any formal clergy within Jewish communities.[44] As Englander has noted:

> In those parts of Eastern Europe from which most immigrants originated, the marriage ceremony was performed in a private house, possibly (but not necessarily) in the presence of a rabbi or other minister of religion. The service was short, the ritual attenuated. The minimal requirement of a valid marriage ceremony was that the bridegroom place a ring on the finger of his bride in the presence of two adult reputable Jewish male witnesses while reciting in Hebrew 'Behold thou art consecrated unto me according to the law of Moses and Israel'. The ketubah (marriage contract) was signed by the parties but not put on record.[45]

Efforts were made to raise awareness of what was required for a legally recognized marriage: the *Manchester Courier* reported that a sermon had been delivered in Yiddish and noted that a 'series of addresses in the minor synagogues' were being delivered to raise awareness of the legal requirements.[46] Measures were also put in place to reduce the cost of getting married in a recognized synagogue.

Even so, the last decades of the nineteenth century and the first few years of the twentieth saw a number of cases coming before the courts involving Jewish marriages that had taken place outside the legal framework. The treatment of these marriages depended on the remedy sought. Deserted wives seeking maintenance from errant husbands in the magistrates' courts received short shrift. Pleas that the ceremony had been conducted in accordance with Jewish law fell on deaf ears: the view was taken that maintenance could only be ordered if there was a lawful marriage, and a lawful marriage required that notice be given to the registrar.[47] In a dispute over inheritance, by contrast, the marriage was upheld on the basis that there was no evidence that the wife had 'knowingly and wilfully' failed to comply with the requirement to give notice.[48] In so deciding, however, the case also confirmed that Jewish marriages were subject to the same annulling provision as all other marriages.

The narrative surrounding such marriages was strikingly similar to that heard in relation to Catholic marriages some decades earlier, albeit with certain differences. Commentators highlighted the foreign origins of these rabbis and the couples being married in this way, but as an explanation rather than as a justification for reform. Many within England's established Jewish communities saw these informal marriages as threatening to the cohesion of Anglo-Jewry and their hard-won status[49]: the Board of Deputies wanted to ensure that marriages were conducted under its purview, rather than seeking to argue for the recognition of those conducted by foreign rabbis.

Commentators also pointed to the impact on deserted wives and children, and to the way in which the non-recognition of informal marriages facilitated bigamy. The *Jewish Chronicle* noted a case that had been brought to the notice of the Board of Deputies in which a man appeared to have gone through no fewer than five illegal marriages. It went on to state, with increasing hyperbole, that

> because he is of our faith … the accomplice of this expert 'bigamist' can screen himself behind the impunity clause: the 'bigamist' himself can even solemnize his own so-called marriages and indulge in his vile propensities *ad lib*: the laws, English and Jewish, are alike rendered powerless against both.[50]

In addition, considerable emphasis was placed on the need for registration. In a desertion case from 1904, an 'assessor' to Dr Adler, Chief Rabbi, confirmed that '[t]here were several forms of ceremony which might be used, and yet be valid as civil marriages; but there must be registration'.[51] What was meant by 'registration' in this context was not the subsequent recording of a marriage in a formal register, but rather giving notice to the superintendent registrar in order to obtain the necessary permission for the marriage to go ahead. This reflected the requirements of the Marriage Act 1836, in that a failure to give notice could render the marriage void, whereas a failure to include it in the register would not.

As well as encouraging couples to marry in a legally recognized ceremony, efforts were made to amend the law. The Marriage Act 1836 had made it an offence for any person to solemnize a marriage in any place other than the registered building specified in the notice of marriage,[52] but since Jewish and Quaker marriages did not have to be conducted in registered buildings they were exempted from its scope. The *Jewish Chronicle* noted that the Board of Deputies wished to surrender this 'doubtful privilege' because it had 'generated serious abuse of the civil and religious law and given every facility for the Irregular Marriages'.[53] In the event, however, no such amendment was made, and with the decline of immigration from Eastern Europe the incidence of religious-only marriages ceased to be a matter for public concern.[54]

This history of religious-only marriages within Jewish communities is of particular importance given the erroneous perception that Jewish marriages have had and continue to have a special status. Under the legislation it is not Jewish marriages that are privileged so much as certain Jewish organizations. The Board of Deputies, the West London Synagogue, and the St John's Wood Synagogue all have the power to certify who is to be responsible for registering marriages. But the mere fact that a marriage is conducted according to Jewish rites does not grant it any right to be registered if it is conducted outside the legal framework. Nor does it guarantee its legal recognition, although the question of what is necessary to bring a Jewish marriage within the scope of the Marriage Act 1949 has not been settled.

Muslim Marriage Practices and the First Mosque Weddings

Had Muslims been present in England and Wales in any significant numbers in the eighteenth century, there is no doubt that they too would have been exempted from the requirements of the Clandestine Marriages Act 1753. What the status of Muslim marriages might have been under the Marriage Act 1836 must be a matter of conjecture, but, if there had been a body that was seen as speaking for the Muslim community as a whole, there is no reason why it would not have been tasked with approving the persons responsible for registering marriages in the same way that the Jewish Board of Deputies was.

As it was, the influence of Muslim marriage practices on the debates about reform in the 1820s and 1830s was largely a negative one. Parallels were drawn between the Unitarians – who were the group primarily interested in reform – and what were termed 'Mahometans', but purely to undermine the case for reform. As one MP pointed out, Unitarians, in denying the divinity of Christ, were far more akin to Muslims than to other Protestant Dissenters.[55] Others denied that there was any hardship to Protestant Dissenters in having to comply with Anglican rites. The Bishop of Chester declared that if he were in a foreign country – 'in a country of Jews, of Catholics, or Mussulmen' – he would 'hold himself bound to comply with the established laws and ceremonies of the country', while maintaining his own convictions and beliefs.[56] Even those arguing in favour of reform invoked Muslim marriage practices in a negative way, with the Earl of Harrowby pointedly asking whether their lordships 'would be satisfied with a marriage ceremony for themselves, in which the name of Mahomet was adjured'.[57]

Clearly, nineteenth-century legislators saw no need to make provision for non-Christian marriages other than those within the established Jewish community. Nor did this change as the century progressed. While an increasing number of Muslims were coming to England and Wales to study and work, their numbers were still in the hundreds rather than the thousands,[58] in contrast to the hundreds of thousands within the different Jewish communities. The majority of Muslims in England and Wales were transitory migrants, employed in dockyards and aboard ships.[59] Towards the end of the century, however, the first mosques were opened – one in Liverpool and another in Woking.[60] And in April 1891, newspapers excitedly reported the celebration of '[t]he first Moslem wedding in England' at the liverpool mosque.[61] This was not, however, a religious-only marriage. The couple in question – a London barrister named Mohammed Almad, and his English bride, Charlotte Fitch – had married on the morning of 18 April in the parish church of St Giles, Camberwell,[62] and had then travelled by train to Liverpool for the ceremony in the mosque that afternoon. The newspaper reports of the wedding convey both a sense of excitement at this novelty and a desire to normalize it. One noted that the service 'was very similar to that with which English people are familiar' while another even claimed that it 'bore much resemblance to the Church of England ceremony'.[63]

It was to be the first of a number of weddings there.[64] *The Crescent* reported the seventh such marriage in 1893, noting that just as a pilgrimage to Mecca 'is one of the events of the life-time of each true believer', so too 'it seems to have become almost adopted as a fundamental principle that, if any Moslem in England desires to be married, he should make a pilgrimage to the Liverpool Mosque, to have the ceremony performed there'.[65]

Despite the fact that reforms to marriage law were being considered again in the 1890s, there would have been nothing in these early mosque marriages to have suggested that legal change was needed to accommodate them. After all, there was no reason in principle why a mosque should not be duly certified as a place of worship and registered for marriages, despite some contemporary comment to the contrary.[66] The initial restriction limiting such certification and registration to Christian places of worship had long disappeared, and a number of Jewish synagogues had chosen to register as a means of escaping the control of the Board of Deputies. It may have been that the failure to register the Liverpool mosque, and the delay in registering the Woking mosque, were due to difficulties in meeting the preconditions for recognition. In order to be registered, a place of worship had to be a separate building, 20 householders were required to certify that it was their usual place of worship, and a fee of £3 had to be paid.[67] Even if these had proved obstacles to registration, Muslims were in effectively the same position as many other small Christian denominations, combining their religious ceremonies with a ceremony in the register office or parish church.

In the early twentieth century, one Muslim religious-only marriage did hit the headlines, but more for its dramatic sequel than for the fact that it was not solemnized according to English law. Clara Casey, a 17-year-old Salford-born dancer, had converted to Islam and gone through a ceremony of marriage with Ben-Bellkassem at the Liverpool mosque. There was a strategic reason for the religious-only ceremony in this case, in that Ben-Bellkassem was already married. He had married Elizabeth Maud Smith at a register office in Lancashire in 1901,[68] the pair having met in her native Glasgow and eloped to England to marry because of opposition from her strict Presbyterian parents. Perhaps it was Clara's working-class background that meant that she was not portrayed as a victim, despite her claims that she had been told that the ceremony in the mosque was 'perfectly valid'.[69] As the *Manchester Courier* reported, the marriage laws and customs of the Islamic authorities in England 'would certainly seem stringent enough in the case of mixed marriages to reduce misunderstanding to a minimum'.[70]

While this was not necessarily an isolated case, the small size of the Muslim population of England and Wales at this time means it is unlikely that any more than a handful of religious-only ceremonies were ever conducted. If anything, the authorities seemed more concerned with the solemnization of legally binding marriages between Indian students and English women.[71] In any case, within a few years the Muslim Institute in Liverpool had foundered, and no more weddings were conducted there. The mosque at Woking similarly closed following the death of its founder. Reopening in 1913, in 1920 it was formally registered for weddings,[72] giving Muslims a place where they could have a legally recognized religious wedding.

Conclusion

Taking the long view shows that religious-only marriages are not unique to Muslim communities. It also shows that many of the earliest Muslim marriages in England and Wales were located within the legal framework, either by being combined with a legally binding ceremony, or, later, by being conducted in a registered mosque.

What is particularly striking is how the same narratives and explanations recur in relation to different religious groups at different times. Catholic, Jewish, and Muslim religious-only marriages have all been linked to the practices of new immigrants. In each case, claims have been made that such religious-only marriages involve the desertion of wives and children, as well as the commission of bigamy. Such commonalities should, however, give us pause. The fact that recent immigrants feature so heavily in the narrative might lead us to conclude that they are uniquely likely to engage in religious-only marriages; it should also lead us to reflect on whether prejudice and unfamiliarity encourage certain assumptions being made about such immigrants. After all, with hindsight we know that some of the wilder estimates as to the number of religious-only marriages – for example, those suggested in relation to the religious-only marriages of Irish Catholics in the 1820s and 1830s – were very far off the mark.

While taking the long view of religious-only marriages may provide some reassurance that this is not a unique or unprecedented issue, it does also raise some uncomfortable questions about how communities may be marginalized and alienated as their marriage practices are brought under the spotlight.

Notes

1   See eg 'Register our Marriage' https://www.registerourmarriage.org/.
2   L Casey, *The Casey Review, A Review into Opportunity and Integration* (London: Department for Communities and Local Government, 2016); Home Office, *The Independent Review into the Application of Sharia Law in England and Wales* (London: Home Office, 2018), Cm 9560.
3   See eg RC Akhtar, 'Unregistered Muslim Marriages: An Emerging Culture of Celebrating Rites and Compromising Rights', in J Miles, P Mody

and R Probert (eds), *Marriage Rites and Rights* (Oxford: Hart, 2015); RC Akhtar, P Nash and R Probert (eds) *Cohabitation and Religious Marriage: Status, Similarities and Solutions* (London: Bristol University Press, 2020); S. Bano, *Muslim Women and Shari'ah Councils: Transcending the Boundaries of Community and Law* (Basingstoke: Palgrave Macmillan, 2012); K O'Sullivan and L Jackson, 'Muslim Marriage (Non) recognition: Implications and Possible Solutions' (2017) 39(1) *JSWFL* 22; R Parveen, 'Religious-Only Marriages in the UK: Legal Positionings and Muslims Women's Experiences' (2018) 6(3) *Sociology of Islam* 316; I Uddin, 'Nikah-Only Marriages: Causes, Motivations and Their Impact on Dispute Resolution and Islamic Divorce Proceedings in England and Wales' (2018) 7(3) *OJLR* 401; V Vora, 'The Problem of Unregistered Muslim Marriage: Questions and Solutions' (2016) *Family Law* 95.

4 R Parveen, 'From Regulating Marriage Ceremonies to Recognising Marriage Ceremonies' in Akhtar, Nash and Probert (eds) *Cohabitation and Religious Marriage*, p 87.

5 *Independent Review*, p 17.

6 See R Probert and S Saleem, 'The Legal Treatment of Islamic Marriage Ceremonies' (2018) 7(3) *OJLR* 376. That is not to say that the law is *experienced* in the same way by different religious groups: see R Probert, R Akhtar and S Blake, *Belief in Marriage: The Evidence for Reforming Weddings Law* (Bristol: Bristol University Press, 2023).

7 For discussion of the status of non-Anglican marriages before 1754, and under the Clandestine Marriages Act 1753, see R Probert, *Marriage Law and Practice in the Long Eighteenth Century: A Reassessment* (Cambridge: Cambridge University Press, 2009), chs 4 and 9.

8 Probert, *Marriage Law and Practice*, ch 6.

9 Clandestine Marriages Act 1753, s 18; Marriage Act 1823, s 31.

10 Probert, *Marriage Law and Practice*, ch 8.

11 Probert, *Marriage Law and Practice*, ch 9.

12 R Probert and L D'Arcy Brown, 'Catholics and the Clandestine Marriages Act of 1753' (2008) 80 *Local Population Studies* 78; Probert, *Marriage Law and Practice*, ch 9.

13 Report on the State of the Irish Poor in Great Britain (1836) PP 34, pp 3, 23, 61–2; S Gallagher, 'Irish Catholic Marriages in the London Lying-in Hospital Records' (1998) 7 *Catholic Ancestor* 102; Royal Commission of Inquiry into Administration and Practical Operation of Poor Laws (1834), PP 44, p 99; App A, pp 103, 105.

14 *Journal of the House of Commons*, 12 June 1823: Petitions of Dr William Poynter and of the Churchwardens, Overseers, and Guardians of the Poor, of the parish of St Luke, Middlesex.

15 *Hansard*, HC Deb 7 August 1834 vol 25 col 1026 (Mr O'Connell).

16 *Journal of the House of Commons*, 12 June 1823: Petition of Dr William Poynter.

17 *Hansard*, HC Deb 7 August 1834 vol 25, col 1026–7. See also the comments by Mr Wilks at col 1026.

18 *Journal of the House of Commons*, 12 June 1823: Petition of the Churchwardens, Overseers, and Guardians of the Poor, of the parish of St Luke, Middlesex.

19 *Hansard*, HC Deb 7 August 1834 vol 25 col 1027.

20 *Morning Chronicle*, 8 August 1834.

21 *Hansard*, HC Deb 7 August 1834 vol 25 col 1027.

22 Roman Catholic Marriages Bills 1832, 1833, 1834.

23 See further R Probert, *Tying the Knot: The Formation of Marriage 1836–2020* (Cambridge: Cambridge University Press, 2021), ch 2.

24 Ibid.

25 Ibid, ch 3.

26 TNA, TS25/873.

27 M Clark, 'Identity and Equality: The Anglo-Jewish Community in the Post-Emancipation Era, 1858–1887 (DPhil thesis, Oxford, 2005), p. 33.

28 On the reasons underpinning this exemption see Probert, *Marriage Law and Practice*, ch 5.

29 Unless they were marrying a non-Jew, in which case this was their only option: see *Jones v Robinson* (1815) 2 Phill Ecc 285; 161 ER 1146.

30 See eg *Vigevena and Silveira v Alvarez* (1794) 1 Hag Con (App) 8n; 161 ER 636.

31 Ibid, at 637.

32 *Lindo v Belisario* (1795) 1 Hag Con 216; 161 ER 530; (1796) 1 Hag Con (App) 7; 161 ER 636.

33 *Lindo v Belisario*; see also *Goldsmid v Bromer* (1798) 1 Hag Con 324; 161 ER 568.

34 Marriage Act 1836, s 2.

35 It was however assumed that witnesses would be present, as provisions relating to registration stated that two witnesses should sign the entry of marriage: Births and Deaths Registration Act 1836, s 31. In practice both groups had their own, more demanding, requirements as to witnesses.

36 Births and Deaths Registration Act 1836, s 30.

37 See Clark, 'Identity and Equality', p 128.

38 Marriage Act 1836, s 2.

39 Marriage Act 1836, s 42.

40 On the foundation of the West London synagogue and its non-recognition by the Board of Deputies see D Katz, *The Jews in the History of England 1485–1850* (Oxford: Clarendon Press, 1994), p 342; D Feldman, *Englishmen and Jews: Social Relations and Political Culture, 1840–1914* (New Haven, CT: Yale University Press, 1994), p 24. On its subsequent legal recognition see Probert, *Tying the Knot*, ch 4.

41 G Alderman, *Modern British Jewry* (Oxford: Clarendon Press, 1992, 1998), pp 3, 74, 119.

42 Clark, 'Identity and Equality', p 163.

43 *Jewish Chronicle*, 28 January 1876.

44 *Jewish Chronicle*, 28 January 1876.

45 David Englander, '*Stille Huppah* (Quiet Marriage) among Jewish Immigrants in Britain' (1992) 34 *Jewish Journal of Sociology* 85, 91.

46 *Manchester Courier*, 14 August 1877.

47 See eg 'A Jewish Marriage Turns to Be No Legal Marriage At All', *Leeds Times*, 1 December 1894; *Birmingham Daily Post*, 4 August 1900; *Yorkshire Evening Post*, 3 May 1901; 'Under the Canopy: Jewish Marriage Practices', *Derby Daily Telegraph*, 3 August 1904.

48 (1899) 15 TLR 250.

49 Englander, '*Stille Huppah*'.

50 *Jewish Chronicle*, 8 April 1892

51 *Derby Daily Telegraph*, 3 August 1904.
52 Marriage Act 1836, s 39.
53 *Jewish Chronicle*, 8 April 1892.
54 Englander, '*Stille Huppah*', 103–4.
55 *Hansard*, HC Deb 25 March 1825 vol 12 col 1237 (Mr Robertson).
56 *Hansard*, HL Deb 2 April 1824 vol 11 col 82.
57 *Hansard*, HL Deb 2 April 1824 vol 11 col 84.
58 R Visram, *Asians in Britain: 400 Years of History* (London: Pluto Press, 2002), p 44.
59 H Ansari, *The Infidel Within: Muslims in Britain since 1800* (London: Hurst, 2004); p 35; S Gilliat-Ray, *Muslims in Britain* (Cambridge: Cambridge University Press, 2010), p 24.
60 Ansari, *The Infidel Within*, p 138.
61 *The Standard*, 20 April 1891. See also *Liverpool Mercury*, 20 April 1891; *Birmingham Daily Post*, 20 April 1891.
62 London Metropolitan Archives, p73/gis/044.
63 *Birmingham Daily Post*, 20 April 1891; *Liverpool Mercury*, 20 April 1891.
64 Ansari, *The Infidel Within*, p 134.
65 *The Crescent*, June 1893.
66 See eg WNM Geary, *The Law of Marriage and Family Relations: A Manual of Practical Law* (London: Adam and Charles Black, 1892), p 89, suggesting that 'a Musssulman mosque or a pagan temple could not be registered for marriages.'
67 Marriage Act 1836, s 18.
68 BMD, Lancaster, Q3 1901.
69 'The Mosque Marriage: Clara Casey Tells Her Story', *Manchester Courier*, 29 May 1905.
70 'Moorish Marriage: Salford Girl at Tangier', *Manchester Courier*, 29 May 1905.
71 For discussion see Sir EJ Trevelyan, 'Marriages between English Women and Natives of British India' (1917) 17 *Journal of Comparative Legislation and International Law* 223; Sir Frederick Robertson, 'The Relations between the English Law and the Personal Law of Indians in England with Special Reference to the Marriage Law' (1918) 18 *Journal of Comparative Legislation and International Law* 242.
72 *London Gazette*, 24 December 1920.

Bibliography

RC Akhtar, 'Unregistered Muslim Marriages: An Emerging Culture of Celebrating Rites and Compromising Rights', in J Miles, P Mody and R Probert (eds), *Marriage Rites and Rights* (Hart, 2015).

RC Akhtar, P Nash and R Probert (eds) *Cohabitation and Religious Marriage: Status, Similarities and Solutions* (Bristol University Press, 2020).

G Alderman, *Modern British Jewry* (Clarendon Press, 1992, 1998).

H Ansari, *The Infidel Within: Muslims in Britain since 1800* (Hurst, 2004).

S Bano, *Muslim Women and Shari'ah Councils: Transcending the Boundaries of Community and Law* (Palgrave Macmillan, 2012).

L Casey, *The Casey Review, A Review into Opportunity and Integration* (Department for Communities and Local Government, 2016).

M Clark, 'Identity and Equality: The Anglo-Jewish Community in the Post-Emancipation Era, 1858–1887' (DPhil thesis, Oxford, 2005).

D Englander, '*Stille Huppah* (Quiet Marriage) among Jewish Immigrants in Britain' (1992) 34 *Jewish Journal of Sociology* 85.

D Feldman, *Englishmen and Jews: Social Relations and Political Culture, 1840–1914* (Yale University Press, 1994).

S Gallagher, 'Irish Catholic Marriages in the London Lying-in Hospital Records' (1998) 7 *Catholic Ancestor* 102.

WNM Geary, *The Law of Marriage and Family Relations: A Manual of Practical Law* (Adam and Charles Black, 1892).

S Gilliat-Ray, *Muslims in Britain* (Cambridge University Press, 2010).

Home Office, *The Independent Review into the Application of Sharia Law in England and Wales* (2018), Cm 9560.

D Katz, *The Jews in the History of England 1485–1850* (Oxford University Press, 1994).

K O'Sullivan and L Jackson, 'Muslim Marriage (Non)recognition: Implications and Possible Solutions' (2017) 39 *JSWFL* 22.

R Parveen, 'Religious-only Marriages in the UK: Legal Positionings and Muslims Women's Experiences' (2018) 6 *Sociology of Islam* 316.

R Parveen, 'From Regulating Marriage Ceremonies to Recognising Marriage Ceremonies', in RC Akhtar, P Nash and R Probert (eds) *Cohabitation and Religious Marriage: Status, Similarities and Solutions* (Bristol University Press, 2020).

R Probert, *Marriage Law and Practice in the Long Eighteenth Century: A Reassessment* (Cambridge University Press, 2009).

R Probert, *Tying the Knot: The Formation of Marriage 1836–2020* (Cambridge University Press, 2021).

R Probert, R Akhtar and S Blake, *Belief in Marriage: The Evidence for Reforming Weddings Law* (Bristol University Press, 2023).

R Probert and L D'Arcy Brown, 'Catholics and the Clandestine Marriages Act of 1753' (2008) 80 *Local Population Studies* 78.

R Probert and S Saleem, 'The Legal Treatment of Islamic Marriage Ceremonies' (2018) 7 *OJLR* 376.

Sir Frederick Robertson, 'The Relations between the English Law and the Personal Law of Indians in England with Special Reference to the Marriage Law' (1918) 18 *Journal of Comparative Legislation and International Law* 242.

Sir EJ Trevelyan, 'Marriages between English Women and Natives of British India' (1917) 17 *Journal of Comparative Legislation and International Law* 223.

I Uddin, 'Nikah-only Marriages: Causes, Motivations and Their Impact on Dispute Resolution and Islamic Divorce Proceedings in England and Wales' (2018) 7 *OJLR* 401.

R Visram, *Asians in Britain: 400 Years of History* (Pluto Press, 2002).

V Vora, 'The Problem of Unregistered Muslim Marriage: Questions and Solutions' (2016) *Family Law* 95.

2 Women and Shari'a Law

The Impact of Soft Legal Pluralism in the UK

Elham Manea

Introduction

The concept of legal pluralism has been a contested subject of re-search. Defined by Jacques Vanderlinden in 1972 as 'the existence within particular society of different legal mechanisms applying to identical institutions',[1] legal pluralism has currently started to attract attention in Europe. The presence of different groups of immigrants has raised the question of whether they should be treated differently according to their religious or original national laws. At the heart of the discourses taking place currently on legal pluralism lays the question of how to balance equality and difference.[2]

Two theoretical points of view in this regard stand out. The first theoretical orientation advocates legal centralism in the state, considers it to be the basic foundation on which liberal-democratic nations rely on, argues for the state's monopoly on legal productions and a monistic conception of law and warns all the same of depriving the state of its capacity as a social actor. It also highlights the negative consequences of legal pluralism on weak groups within the minorities, such as women and children; and insists on equal protection of rights within one society through the application of a 'single and comprehensive vision of justice'. The second theoretical standpoint argues for legal pluralism, maintains that legal centralism is more relevant within a Western model jurisprudence, that it ignores the experience of non-Western nations. Accordingly, legal pluralism indicates that state law is only one of many levels, and it means a plurality of social fields and produces of norms, which are in partial interaction with each other. It also insists that legal pluralism is the adequate system that guarantees the protection of minorities' rights and their entitlement to be different.[3]

This discussion, while concerning itself with describing legal and social realities in Western and non-Western states, has rarely touched

DOI: 10.4324/9781003090410-3

on the political function of legal pluralism. It also has seldom elaborated on how legal pluralism contributes to the rise of what one could call parallel or closed societies/communities, and most importantly how the interaction between the two and the application of legal pluralism reflect on the rights of members of these parallel communities within the state, especially from a human rights perspective.

From a theoretical point of view, however, it is important to differentiate between two levels of perspectives:

a   de jure level where different types of legal systems are applied by the state to different ethnic communities within its boundaries. Accordingly, the state itself seems to designate these communities as distinct and different, as with the case, for instance, of religious minorities in Islamic states, native Indians in the US and Canada, and members of ethnic minorities/migrants in Britain and Germany;

b   de facto level where different (written and/or unwritten) rules of behaviour and values seem to distinguish a community from its general society.

The changing demographic structures with Western European societies gave a new push to this discussion. Waves of immigrants moved to Western European societies in the 1950s and 1960s for different reasons: some came because of economic reasons (workers from Southern Europe and Turkey helping in rebuilding Germany during its years of economic boom) and others as members of previous colonies of their hosted states (North Africans in France and Indians and Pakistanis in the UK). Another wave of migration followed in the 1980s, 1990s, and the first two decades of this millennium as a result of the wars and political upheavals, e.g. Yugoslavia, Sri Lanka, Somalia, Iraq, Syria, etc.

Some of the new groups of immigrants started to organise themselves along ethnic and religious lines and in some cases created separate cultural and social entities, sometimes functioning with different cultural norms than those prevalent in the society. The debate on parallel societies and/or the construction of 'parallel societies' as an 'image of the other' has been debated in Germany since the German sociologist Wilhelm Heitmeyer first used the term in the early 1990s and was later criticised by Wolfgang Kashuba.[4]

Within the UK, three general groups have been calling for the introduction of forms of Islamic law, shari'a, into British legal system:

1   Islamic and Islamist organisations. The terms Islamic and Islamist have different meanings. *Islamic* organisations often represent a traditional if not conservative reading of Islam, are led by individuals of traditional/conservative religious background, and often seek to impose a religious identity on 'Muslim community' members. *Islamist* organisations espouse a political agenda that aims to Islamise migrant communities of Islamic faith. Some Islamic organisations have members who espouse the ideology of Islamism and some do not. Often they work together and support each other's religious demands. Together they often claim to be the sole representative and voice of 'Muslim communities' and their experts on their 'needs'.

2   High officials, lawyers, judges, or political personalities seem to be concerned about how Muslim communities are becoming integrated in their respective countries, and consider the move towards shari'a law inevitable if Muslims are to integrate 'successfully'. Dr Rowan Williams, the former archbishop of Canterbury, is one famous example; another is Marion Boyd, Ontario's attorney general. Some of these people may be calling for soft legal pluralism for pragmatic political reasons. They earnestly believe that combating Islamic extremism – a serious problem in Britain – will require giving small concessions to the Muslim community, such as allowing them to live by Islamic family laws. Britain's former Lord Chief Justice Baron Phillips of Worth Matravers (equivalent to the chief justice of the US Supreme Court) made a comment that might be understood in this light. It is no coincidence that Islamic and Islamist organisations in Britain make the same argument: 'Give us Islamic law in family affairs to curb extremism'.[5]

3   Academics in a range of social science fields, specifically legal anthropology, law, and sociology, who are leading a theoretical and intellectual discourse about the state: does it have a monopoly on legal productions and norms, on minorities and multiculturalism? They maintain that legal centralism is a Western model of jurisprudence, that it ignores the experience of non-Western nations. They blame colonial powers for depriving people in developing countries of access to their own traditional and customary laws, imposing their version of positive law on their colonies. They cite a 'more complex' relationship between law and society, one 'where law is conceptualised as more plural, not located entirely in the state'.[6] Accordingly, legal pluralists hold that state law is only one of many levels of law; their idea implies a plurality

of social fields and producers of norms, which interact somewhat with each other. They also insist that legal pluralism is an adequate system that guarantees the protection of minorities' rights and of their entitlement to be different.[7] They argue that an even-handed sensitivity to difference requires an abandonment of the formal vision of equality, one that assumes that all citizens are inherently identical. Instead, the legal system should take cognisance of the identity and values of different sections of the population, no matter how distinctive these values maybe.[8] Within the British discourse on *weak* legal pluralism, some strong advocates are the American John R. Bowen, who is Dunbar-Van Cleve Professor in Sociocultural Anthropology at Washington University in St. Louis; Roger Ballard, the director of the Centre for Applied South Asian Studies; and Tariq Modood, a British-Pakistani professor of sociology, politics, and public policy at the University of Bristol.

Members of these three groups are often of the opinion that weak legal pluralism is just one out of many instruments for resolving conflicts, and that it is an extension of a right already given to the Jewish minority: a right to arbitration tribunals in a system called Beth Din. And, they say, since the Jews already have it, why not Muslims as well?

They emphasise that this instrument of conflict resolution is voluntary, that they only support it with safeguards that ensure respect for human rights, especially for women's rights. Accordingly, if a member of a religious minority does not want to be ruled by these laws, all she or he has to do is to opt out and leave the community.

And they often argue that the Western legal tradition, which is based on legal centralism and state monopoly over legal productions and a monistic conception of law (the basic foundation on which liberal-democratic nations are instituted) is Euro-American centric and ignores the experience of non-Western nations.

Those calling for soft legal pluralism in the UK are often shaped by strong or weak cultural relativism. The strong cultural relativists hold that 'culture is the *principal* source of the validity of a moral right or rule [...] the presumption is that rights (and other social practices, values, and moral rules) are culturally determined'.[9] The weak cultural relativists, on the other hand, assert that 'culture may be an *important* source of the validity of a moral right or rule. Universality is initially presumed, but the relativity of human nature, communities, and rights serves as a check on potential excesses of universalism.'[10]

Absent from this plead for the introduction of Islamic law is the actual experience with legal pluralism in non-Western countries specifically with its often grave political and human rights consequences.[11] Also absent is clarity about the type of Islamic law being used in this so-called method of conflict resolution. No one considers the social context within which this law is being implemented. The diversity and multitude of positions towards Islamic law, the critical discourse in Islamic countries among civil society actors and intellectuals, and their attempts to change Islamic laws: none of this seems to be relevant to this discourse. Indeed, the discourse is often very academic and theoretical, ignoring the settings or circumstances within which women are living in closed societies. It is as if Muslim women, Muslims, and Islam itself had been crafted and constructed separate from their historical, political, social, and religious contexts. Based on fieldwork conducted by the author in 2013 and numerous visits later, the results of which were published in a book in 2016 with the title *Women and Shari'a Law: The Impact of Legal Pluralism in the UK*, this chapter presents the context and consequences of the application of Islamic law in the UK Shari'a Councils and Muslim Arbitration Councils.

Legal Pluralism in the UK

The UK allows the application of Islamic law in family affairs in shari'a councils and Muslim Arbitration Tribunals. Muslims are not the only group that resort to their religious laws. Jewish and Hindu laws are used as well. My research, however, focuses on the Muslim separate legal system that exists.

The 2001 census estimated that the Muslim population in the UK is 1.6 million, or 2.7 per cent of the total population. Between 2004 and 2008, according to the Office of National Statistics, the number grew by more than 500,000 to 2.4 million, a growth rate ten times that of the rest of British society. In 2011 the number rose to more than 2.7 million. Nearly half of those people were born in the UK.[12] In 2017 the UK Muslim population rose to 4.1 million, or 6.3 per cent of the total population.[13]

Application of Islamic law takes two forms, in the Shari'a Councils and in the Muslim Arbitration Councils. The number of Shari'a Councils is unknown and ranges from 35 to 85 councils.[14] These are not subject to any supervision, they deny access to legal advice and legal assistance, appeals to their decisions are not possible, and their focus is on family disputes. The majority of their applicants are women, who seek a religious divorce from their husbands. Muslim

Arbitration Tribunals apply Islamic law under the British Arbitration Act of 1996 and therefore their judgments are legally binding. Both parties must agree first to arbitration. There are indications that these tribunals, just like the councils, have turned into parallel legal structures. They arbitrate on family disputes, domestic violence, and even in cases of child abuse.[15]

The next sections will address the following three questions: what is the profile of women turning to shari'a courts? Why do they turn to these courts? And finally what type of law is being used in these courts?

Profiles of Women Turning to Shari'a Courts

The classification below is based on two sources. The first is a six-month examination of cases that went to trial conducted by Salma Dean, a survivor of a forced marriage and a barrister working on human rights; she worked on Baroness Cox's team on the Equality Bill. The second source is Charlotte Proudman, a human rights barrister who researched the councils, provided a report in support of the Equality Bill, and shared some of the cases she addressed. Based on these two sources, three types of cases can be identified.[16]

First Type of Case: Religious Divorce

A woman whose marriage is forced or arranged seeks a religious divorce because she believes that a civil divorce does not suffice, as people have told her that under Muslim law she is not divorced.

Within this category is another subgroup: mainly first- or second-generation Muslim women, who were born and brought up in England and often have a strong Muslim identity. Others are women who converted to Islam and took on an Islamic mantle. For this group it is crucial to have a religious divorce, just as they desired a religious marriage.

Sonia Shah-Kazemi and Samia Bano each conducted studies on shari'a councils, interviewing 20 to 25 women each. They both highlighted how important it was to these women to get a religious divorce, as they consider that doing so is 'part of their religious identity'.[17]

Second Type of Case: Marriage Outside of the UK

These marriages may be either forced or arranged. The ceremony may have taken place in Pakistan, Bangladesh, or India, and no civil marriage followed in the UK. Under international private law, the UK recognises a marriage conducted outside of the country and considers it legally binding, and therefore it is legally possible to dissolve it. Many women do not know this and think that the only place they can get help ending their marriage is a shari'a court.

Within this category are those who come to England on a spousal visa, often marrying a cousin or a member of a clan living in the UK. Usually they do not speak English, they have little if any formal education, and they are not aware of their legal rights in England. They live under the patriarchal regime in the family household, often in poverty in a ghettoised area of England. Women in this category 'genuinely believe that the community is the only option they have in England; they are not aware of the wider society in England'.[18]

Third Type of Case: UK Marriage Not Under Civil Law

Women in this category had a religious marriage but failed to register it. Such marriages, called *nikahs*, are not recognised under civil law, so these women must go to a shari'a court to get a divorce. This category is prevalent among British Muslim women, with dire legal consequences.

In 2017 Channel 4 conducted the largest survey to date on Muslim unregistered marriages.[19] The survey covered 923 Muslim women and was

> carried out by 20 female Muslim community researchers between December 2016 and September 2017 through face-to-face and phone interviews. Four fifths of those interviewed were born in the UK, and 99 per cent had a religious ceremony. 60.1 per cent of those said that they did not have a civil marriage ceremony in addition to their religious marriage. Over one quarter (28.2 %) of those in religious-only marriages believed, incorrectly, that they were legally married in the UK and therefore had the legal protections that entails.[20]

The failure to register an Islamic religious marriage is considered a widespread problem in the UK – alarming to the extent that the BBC reported on it and women's organisations launched campaigns to alert women about the consequences of not registering their marriages. Cassandra Balchin, the late president of the Muslim Women's Network, explained that *nikahs* are a matter of concern because the woman has little recourse to justice if she experiences discord in the relationship or her husband dies.[21]

There are many reasons why women fail to register their marriages. The most common is ignorance about the legal status of religious marriage, but sometimes women want to test a relationship before committing to a real civil marriage. Often the situation results when the husband makes a deliberate attempt to trick his wife out of registering a civil marriage and thus enjoying the rights that civil law affords to women.[22]

In her study *Untying the Knot*, Sonia Shah-Kazemi examined a total of 287 case files in one shari'a council in Ealing, West London. She found that 57 per cent of the women had a religious Islamic marriage but did not register it in the UK as required by civil law (not all of these religious marriages took place in the UK); 27 per cent who had religious marriages in the UK did not register them.[23]

Samia Bono also examined cases in various shari'a councils in the UK for her *Muslim Women and Shari'a Councils*. Most of those cases involved women whose religious marriages were not registered. This was not a matter of the women making a deliberate decision. In fact, the majority of these women expected that their religious marriages would be registered after they completed the religious ceremony and consummated the marriage. But some husbands simply refused to register, and thus formalise, the marriage as required by civil law. Bano concludes that it would be difficult to ignore the 'relations of power and the gendered cultural norms and values' that underline the decisions made by many husbands not to formalise the marriage. These women are left with a violation of their trust and a loss of decision-making and autonomy in the marriage.[24]

Sometimes the husband has another motive for refusing to register the marriage: he is entering into a polygamous marriage.

In an interview with the BBC, Dr Ghayasuddin Siddiqui, a British Muslim leader in the UK, and a founding trustee of the Muslim Institute and of British Muslims for Secular Democracy, expressed his concern about the exploitation some women are subjected to. Their partners promise them a civil wedding after the religious marriage, and then refuse to go ahead with it after consummating the marriage:

> This allows Muslim men to control their wives because they can threaten to leave them and end the Islamic marriage by just saying the words 'divorce, divorce, divorce' to her. It also enables some men to commit polygamy. I know of cases where men have taken on several wives because they have just had the *nikah* with each partner.[25]

The rise of fundamentalist interpretations of Islam within some closed communities, some of my interviewees contend, has mainstreamed polygamy as part of an 'Islamic way of life'. It has also led 'women to be misled' that a religious marriage, a *nikah*, is the 'proper Muslim way'.[26] When they face troubles in their marriage they discover that they are left with no protection and are forced to go to a shari'a court.

Why Women Turn to the Shari'a Courts

The types of cases I outlined above, and the reasons why women turn to shari'a courts, highlight the social context within which they are often operating – a patriarchal order. Though their context may be similar, their backgrounds are diverse. Some are educated, and independent, with their own income, while many others have only a minimum of formal education, and are economically inactive and poverty stricken. Some are living in closed communities, while a few others are not constrained by such structures; this is especially true of converts.

Yet despite their diversity they share one common feature: what they often want is a *religious divorce*. This is important. They are not interested in mediation or arbitration; they want to end their marriage and get a religious divorce. The fact that the majority of women going to the shari'a courts have not registered or formalised their religious marriage according to civil law only highlights the legal loopholes that compel these women to seek the assistance of the shari'a courts. Once they go there, they enter into an inherently discriminatory process, in which they are pushed to seek mediation instead of divorce. Some are even forced to concede the rights they would be afforded by civil law, as their only means to get the religious divorce they desperately seek.

At the three shari'a councils I visited in London and Birmingham, the people I met all confirmed that women who resort to the shari'a councils are seeking a religious divorce.

Sister Sabah, the administrative coordinator of the Family Support Service at the Islamic Shari'a Council in Birmingham told me that nine out of ten cases coming to the council are from women applying for divorce: 'obviously [...], if a man wants a divorce they can give it to themselves'. Women are given a choice: 'if they want to have a divorce privately, they are able to [be referred to a mosque]; if they want a certificate, then they have to follow the procedure'.[27]

The procedures will involve visiting the council's Family Support Service and Counseling Clinic, where female counsellors will listen to the case of the individual or couple. The counsellors will suggest reconciliation as a matter of Islamic principle. If the person insists on divorce, their case will be given a number. Once the case files are ready, the case will be put forward to the shari'a council, which will consider the case and deliver its final verdict on whether to grant the divorce, called a *talaq*, or a *khula*, a divorce initiated by the woman.[28]

Sheikh Mohammad Talha Bokhari, the coordinator of the Shari'a Council and one of its members, confirmed Sister Sabah's account. Asked about the types of cases that come to the council, he said they do not get many marriage cases; their mosque has a marriage bureau that deals with such cases. Rather, the council deals with divorce cases; in most of them, 'the wife does not want to live with him and the husband does not want to give her a divorce'.[29]

Dr Mohammad Shahoot Kharfan, the imam of the Muslim Welfare House in London, said that most of the cases he deals with are either to contract a marriage or to issue a divorce. What he usually does first is try mediation between the two partners; when this does not succeed he issues a divorce.[30]

Salim Leham, the legal director of the Muslim Welfare House in London, explained to me that most of those coming to the centre are refugees of Arab or Somali backgrounds. Very often they do not speak English and need assistance. His role is to help them in their communications with the local authorities. When it concerns family cases, specifically issues of *talaq* and *khula*, people are referred to the imam, in this case Dr Kharfan. Sometimes Leham translates for him if the applicant is a convert who does not speak Arabic. He added that the 'sheikh gives the Islamic perspective, but we live in a state that is not Muslim; its law should be implemented. So we explain the British divorce process to them, [...] and help them in the court system'.[31]

On the other hand, Sheikh Dr Suhaib Hasan, of the Islamic Shari'a Council in Leyton, stated that his council was created in 1982 to 'guide the Muslim community in all matters'; later the council recognised that there was a 'great field still not filled by any Muslim organisation: the field of matrimonial problems of *talaq* and *khula*. So then we said, all right, let us fill this vacuum'. Asked about the type of service the council is offering – mediation, arbitration, or family counselling services – Sheikh Dr Hasan answered:

> We receive a lot of cases of women seeking *khula*. Now the very same woman might go to civil court as well. And civil courts do not try to mediate, they do not try to reconcile, but they try to

give the decision regarding the case which is presented to them. But that is not the case with us. Here, whenever a woman applies for a divorce, we treat it as a case of *khula*, in which the man has to be persuaded to give his consent. If he is not ready, if he is not willing to give a *khula*, then it is not a proper *khula*. Then it becomes our responsibility as *qadis* [judges] to dissolve the marriage.

So in this way, we have to have a joint meeting for husband and wife, and when they come, we try to mediate between them. So this is part of our policy, that we should try to mediate between the two of them and try to explore if there are any avenues in which they can come together, they can minimise their differences, and they can live together. We ask a woman if she has any conditions, please lay down these conditions, and we say to the man, if you comply with these conditions, we will give you still another chance, two or three months, and if the man does not comply with these conditions, then we will award the woman the divorce she is seeking.

So we do try mediate in each and every case, except when it becomes very clear that the woman is a victim of violence, and there is no room for reconciliation at all. Then and only then we take the decision ourselves to dissolve the marriage because the man does not want a divorce, but if he is willing to divorce then the matter is very easy.[32]

Hence, mediation is almost always offered as an obligatory part of the process even if the woman has a clear objective of obtaining a religious divorce. This may lead to situations where women are forced to enter into mediation.

Sonia Shah-Kazemi and Samia Bano, in their two separate studies, have highlighted that the single most important reason why women turn to shari'a councils is to get a religious divorce – not a desire to save their marriage or enter mediation.[33] Shah-Kazemi, who favours the use of shari'a councils, asked her interviewees about their views on mediation. All talked about the positive aspect of mediators coming from backgrounds like their own. However, women who came from small, close-knit communities (from different regions in the UK) did express their concerns about confidentiality within the community. Only one interviewee had actually gone through the mediation process. When mediation concerns their children, the positive attitude towards mediation evaporates.

Shah-Kazemi recognised that women who come to the Shari'a Council have made up their mind about the divorce. One of her interviewees put it this way:

> [The situation was] too far gone; if there had been any doubt in my mind I would not have started the procedure [...] I had thought about it: 'Is there any hope in this?'[34]

Samia Bano, who extensively studied these mechanisms, has observed that in some cases women were encouraged to reconcile even if they did not wish to do so. She is very much aware of the troubling context within which mediation takes place: it is riddled with dynamics of power emphasising what is described as the woman's divinely ordained obligation. It is also male dominated, and often imbued with conservative interpretations about the position of women in Islam.[35]

Bamo describes one of the troubling findings of her study: ten of her interviewees reported that they had been 'coaxed' into participating in the reconciliation sessions with their husbands even though they were reluctant to do so. More troubling still, four of these women had existing injunctions against their husbands on the grounds of domestic violence and yet they were urged to sit only a few feet away from these men during the reconciliation sessions.[36]

Bano came to this conclusion:

> Empirical findings in this study confirm the existence of intra-group inequalities and that Shari'ah councils construct boundaries for group membership that rely upon traditional interpretations of the role of women in Islam, primarily as wives, mothers and daughters. Under such conditions the multicultural accommodation of Muslim family law in Britain can lead to violations of human rights for Muslim women. In effect this privatised form of religious arbitration means the shifting of state regulation to the private domain thereby giving religious leaders greater power to dictate acceptable patterns of behaviour.[37]

Similarly, Charlotte Proudman, who provided evidence in support of Baroness Cox's bill, said that in all the cases she examined, women went to shari'a courts to end their marriages. Yet more often than not, these women were pushed to enter mediation in a process that was misogynist and gender discriminatory. Proudman not only profiled cases she dealt with personally in her capacity as a lawyer. She also documented testimonies provided by nine reputable Muslim and women's organisations working within the communities, which handled cases of women turning to shari'a courts.[38]

Their accounts are important in illustrating the patriarchal social context of these women, the social control and pressure they endure while seeking to receive their religious divorce, and the lack of legal knowledge, combined with the system's legal loopholes, that are driving them to shari'a councils. Two testimonies are worth mentioning.

The first is of Jasvinder Sanghera, the president of Karma Nirvana – a renowned registered charity – which supports victims and survivors of forced marriage and honour-based abuse. Sanghera provides expert evidence and opinions in family law matters to UK courts of law. She gave this testimony:

> Many women telephoning Karma Nirvana are calling to ask how to obtain a shari'a divorce. Karma Nirvana supports them with their application, often providing women with a letter of support. Once women begin the shari'a divorce process, the shari'a councils soon pressurise vulnerable and marginalised women to reconcile their marriage. Family members also become involved further adding to the pressure these women are under to return to the matrimonial home regardless of the abuse that they have, and will continue to, suffer. Where women refuse to return to their husband, shari'a Councils have insisted that women return their children to their husbands. Once the child is returned to its father there is a high risk that the child will be abducted.[39]

The Henna Foundation, a national registered charity committed to strengthening families in Muslim communities, highlighted the legal misinformation that leaves these women vulnerable. Over the past 12 years one-third of Henna's work involved Muslim women who were seeking an Islamic divorce and clarity on their Muslim marriage:

> The lack of regulation and accountability of the Councils has caused undue stress and pressure particularly on Muslim women. This can be illustrated in the lack of acceptance of decree absolutes [civil divorce] as a valid and finalised divorce for Muslim women. A number of renowned scholars have made it clear that a decree absolute [civil divorce] is sufficient to fulfil the requirements of an Islamic divorce and technically Muslim women need not obtain a Shari'a Council divorce. However due to community pressure, lack of understanding of divorce, and also for peace of mind, a large majority of Muslim women will apply for an Islamic

divorce once given their decree absolute. The lack of understanding on the issue of divorce is particularly concerning as there are religious leaders and ex-husbands etc. who exploit this and tell vulnerable Muslim women that they are still married in Islam and that they have to continue to perform their duty/role as a wife.[40]

The above descriptions paint a picture of what I call an *anthropological version of the law*. I define it as a version of law void of any historical, political, or even legal context. Again, it is at play here in the contexts described above. Women are lost in a confusing system that persistently fails to address their needs.

Women are resorting to the shari'a courts because they need to obtain a religious divorce, but the need is complicated by three factors.

First, most women are ignorant about the legal status of marriage and divorce. On the one hand, most of these women are unaware that a marriage conducted outside of the UK is accepted as legally binding back in Britain. They can therefore obtain a civil divorce with the protection that comes with it. On the other hand, most are also unaware that a British civil divorce is religiously accepted as a valid divorce.

Second, the woman's religious marriage contracted in the UK may not be registered. As I described above, many women who seek divorce have contracted only religious marriages in the UK and have failed to register them. They need a divorce and to get that divorce they turn to the shari'a councils.

Third, the fundamentalist interpretation of Islam is being mainstreamed. The rise of fundamentalist interpretations of Islam, such as those in Salafi Islam, has mainstreamed and propagated the false assumption within closed UK communities that a Muslim woman is only divorced through an Islamic divorce. This opinion was strongly articulated by Haitham al-Haddad, a former member of Shari'a Council, Leyton, who warned against accepting the 'judgment of non-Muslims' in a fatwa he issued in July 2010. He insisted that a 'divorce issued by the civil court in response to the wife's request is neither a valid divorce nor legitimate marriage dissolution'.[41]

Al-Haddad's opinion is in fact a fringe opinion – an extreme one. It contradicts the actual practice in many Islamic countries, including Pakistan, Bangladesh, Tunisia, and Morocco, which do accept a civil divorce as a valid divorce. Sohail Akbar Warraich and Cassandra Balchin demonstrated this legal practice in their report *Recognising the un-Recognised*; they say that cases coming before courts in Bangladesh and Pakistan involving a British civil divorce always involve custody and property disputes, and neither party challenges the actual fact of the divorce.[42]

Al-Haddad's opinion also stands at odds with classical Islamic ju-risprudence. In fact, Rashad Ali points out that Muslim scholars have traditionally advised Muslims to obtain divorces from courts within the legal system where they live. Such divorces would be legitimate divorces both on religious grounds and according to the law of the land. This position is not novel – it is part of classical Islamic jurispru-dence and has long been advocated by pre-modern scholars for Mus-lims living in areas which have a majority non-Muslim population or even where non-Muslims were judges in Muslim-majority countries. Accordingly, it is religiously, morally, and legally binding upon Mus-lims to adopt the prevailing legal norms and standards within their own contractual undertakings. One leading contemporary authority on Islamic law, Sheikh Abdullah Bin Mahfudh Bin Bayyah, explicitly states that you are married and divorced according to the laws of the country where you live.[43]

He is not alone in this. The Birmingham Council abides by this rule. Indeed, Sheikh Mohammad Talha Bokhari, the coordinator of that shari'a council and one of its members, explained to me that if a woman came with a civil divorce, she would not need a religious divorce from the council: 'Because when the [civil] divorce has come, issued from the civil court, then she is done. That is a divorce.'[44]

Supporters of Shari's councils reject this solid theological position and the modern practice of legal systems in Islamic countries; instead they argue for an *anthropological version of Islamic law*, demand-ing that a parallel legal order of shari'a courts be integrated into the Western legal system. This is a misrepresentation of the issue. Women are not seeking religious arbitration; what they need is a procedural measure that allows them to get a religious divorce without having to go to a religious court. The British authorities have so far failed to address this problem out of an absurd sense of political correctness. There are specific policy measures that can address the issue but doing so will require political will. I will describe them in the conclusion.

The Type of Islamic Law Implemented in UK Shari'a Councils and Muslim Arbitration Tribunal

I define shari'a by the way it is being implemented in Islamic states and within Muslim family laws. I see it as a selection from the corpus of legal opinions of jurists developed over the course of Islamic his-tory, especially between the seventh and tenth centuries.

Looking at shari'a from this perspective will highlight its problem-atic nature, for we are not considering its theoretical potential to pro-vide justice. What we are in fact looking at is its actual implementation and hence its obvious limitations and how it contravenes *modern* concepts of human rights. What matters is how it is being interpreted and used today, not how it could be used a century from now.

I deliberately used the word modern above, because the jurisprudence suggested and under consideration was developed between the seventh and tenth centuries. This historical period, early in the development of Islam as a whole, shaped its content and its perception of women's role in society, and is reflected in its worldview of what constitutes a human and who can enjoy human rights.

In fact, if we look at the actual corpus of Islamic law, human rights can be defined as the privilege 'only of persons of full legal capacity'. A person of full legal capacity is 'a living human being of mature age, free [not a slave], and of Moslem faith'. Under this definition, others who lived in the Islamic state, including non-Moslems and slaves, were 'only partially protected by law or had no legal capacity at all'.[45] This definition was formulated in 1946 by Majid Khadurri, an Iraqi-born American academic recognised as a leading authority on Islamic law and the modern political history of the Middle East.

More than 50 years later, that definition was qualified by Abdullahi Ahmed An-Na'im, a leading Sudan-born American authority on Islamic law and human rights. In 1990, he accepted Khadurri's statement as 'substantially accurate' and added a qualification concerning the status of Muslim women. He acknowledged that Muslim women 'have full legal capacity under Shari'a in relation to civil and commercial law matters', but they 'do not enjoy human rights on an equal footing with Muslim men under Shari'a'.[46]

What does that mean?

It means that in addition to creating a stratified citizenry dominated by free male Muslims, the way shari'a dealt with the status of women was often contradictory, offering women some rights but withholding many others, while maintaining the notion that the Muslim man is the keeper and guardian of the Muslim woman.

In general, one can discern two levels of statements in the Qur'an regarding women's status. The first level treats women and men as equal before God – that is, in the afterlife. For example, one verse states: 'Whoso does evil will be requited only with the like of it; but whoso does good, whether male or female, and is a believer – these will enter the paradise; they will be provided therein without measure' (Qur'an 40:41).

Qur'anic verses at the second level place women at a legal disadvantage. These are the statements on issues of family and sexual relations, rules of marriage, divorce, custody, maintenance, inheritance, and testimony – that is, rights within this life. On these issues, Qur'anic verses reflect the social tribal patriarchal context of the seventh-century Arabian Peninsula, specifically the city of Medina. They favoured men and accorded women a lower and dependent legal status. From this we see the clear inconsistencies on the status of women between the Qur'anic provisions and the modern statements on human rights, such as the 1948 Universal Declaration of Human Rights (UDHR) and the Convention on the Elimination of All Forms of Discrimination Against Women (CEDAW).

Let us start with the first part of An-Na'im's qualification. He says that under shari'a, a Muslim woman has full legal capacity in relation to matters of civil and commercial law. This means that she can own property as a separate person and that when she marries she can keep her name. Hence when I married, I kept my family name, Manea, and did not take my husband's name. Nor did he take over whatever property I had. It remained in my possession. From this perspective, a Muslim woman is treated as an individual.

Yet An-Na'im is also correct to state that, under shari'a, Muslim women do not enjoy human rights on an equal footing with Muslim men. In fact shari'a laws contravene various provisions of human rights conventions, specifically the UDHR and the CEDAW mentioned above.

Human rights conventions are clear in their statements about the equality of man and woman. The essence of their worldview is expressed by Article One of the 1948 UDHR: that all human beings are born free and equal in dignity and rights. This principle paved the ground for Article 16 of the same declaration and Article 16 of CEDAW. Both articles envisioned marriage and family relations as an equal partnership that would be entered, shared, and dissolved by both man and woman on an equal footing. Marriage should be entered by two persons of full age, with their free and full consent, without any limitation due to race, nationality, or religion. The spouses should have same rights and responsibilities with regard to guardianship of children, and the same personal rights as husband and wife, including the right to choose a family name, a profession, and an occupation. And both spouses should have the same rights in respect of the ownership, acquisition, management, administration, enjoyment, and disposition of property, whether free of charge or for a valuable consideration.

This is not the case in the worldview of classical Islamic law: woman is part of a hierarchical social structure dominated by the man at the top; and as a legal person the woman is controlled before her marriage by her male guardian and after marriage by her husband.

The rules regarding marriageable age and guardianship make child marriages and forced marriages possible, and rules on divorce and maintenance rights discriminate against the wife.

In fact, the Islamic law's view towards the position of the wife within marriage can be easily discerned by considering the legal term used for marriage – a term, remember, that was developed in the Middle Ages.

In Islamic law, the term for marriage is *nikah*, which literally means carnal union. Jurists describe *nikah* as 'an agreement, which results in the lawful enjoyment of a woman'.[47] The reference to enjoyment applies only to the husband, because that right belongs especially and pre-eminently to him. In fact, the husband is entitled to intercourse with his wife at his pleasure. On the other hand, two realities restrict the wife's right to enjoyment. First, she has no right to claim intercourse with her husband, except for one time after marriage, and second, she may have to share him with other wives.[48]

This perception of marriage is not theoretical. In fact it has been used repeatedly in various Islamic and Arab family laws, such as those in Yemen, Kuwait, and Syria. All of them state in their first article that marriage is a legal union or a contract that gives the man the legal permission to access his wife sexually. The only time this definition has changed has been in genuine attempts to reform the classic Islamic law on family relations. For example, the Moroccan Family Code of 2004 states, 'Marriage is a legal contract by which a man and a woman mutually consent to unite in a common and enduring conjugal life.'[49]

Aside from the legal definition of marriage, classical Islamic law does not envision marriage and family relations as an equal partnership between man and woman. In the paragraphs below I summarise the common provisions regarding marriage and divorce.

Marriage

- Age of marriage: A Muslim man or a woman must be of sound mind and must have attained puberty to be considered legally eligible for marriage. In classical Islamic law, puberty occurs with the physical signs of maturity such as the emission of semen for boys and menstruation for girls.[50]
- Guardianship: In contracting a marriage, male guardianship is necessary. The established interpretations of Islamic jurisprudence

schools insist that a woman cannot marry without the consent of her male guardian. A guardian handles all kinds of affairs for both his male and female wards, including contracting marriage. When the ward is a male, the guardianship ceases when the boy reaches puberty. For a girl, however, a guardian has the power to impose a marriage on a virgin girl without her knowledge or consent.[51] If she contracts a marriage without her guardian's consent, the marriage is not valid. If she was divorced, her consent, in addition to that of the guardian, is necessary to contract the marriage.

The one crucial exception to this rule in Sunni Islam occurs in the Hanafite school of jurisprudence; it is also present in Shi'a jurisprudence. Guardianship is required when the girl is not of age, that is, has not yet reached puberty. But once she reaches puberty, she is allowed to contract her marriage without her guardian's consent.[52] However, under Hanafite jurisprudence, if the guardian is not satisfied with her choice of husband, he has the right to demand that marriage be annulled on the basis of lack of *kafaa*: social equality. The concept of *kafaa*, literally suitability, gives the guardian the right to dissolve and annul a marriage, if he considers the groom/husband not to be fit or suitable.

- **Polygamy**: A Muslim man may be married to up to four wives at the same time but a Muslim woman can only be married to one man at a time. A Muslim man may marry a Christian or a Jewish woman, but a Muslim woman may not marry a non-Muslim man.

Divorce

- A Muslim man may divorce his wife, or any of his wives, by unilateral repudiation, *talaq*, without having to give any reasons or justify his action to any person or authority. When he divorces his wife by uttering the word three times, the divorce is considered irrevocable: *bain*. In order to return to him, she must first marry a different man and get a divorce from the new husband.
- A Muslim woman can obtain a divorce in three ways: (a) by gaining the consent of her husband; (b) by getting a judicial decree for limited specific grounds/harms; or (c) by *khula*. This means a divorce sanctioned by a judge, but she must give up her financial rights to gain it.
- A woman divorced by her husband must observe a waiting period (*iddah*), normally lasting three months. During this period she cannot marry another man.

- A divorce in which the word is uttered fewer than three times is revocable (*raji'i*). So even if a woman gets a divorce, her husband may change his mind. During the waiting period, he has the right to return her to his household against her will and he need not sign another marriage contract. One reference on *fiqh* explained this rule this way: 'until the period of *iddah* has elapsed, the repudiation is revocable (*raji'i*), and the husband may resume conjugal relations with his wife, if he be so inclined, by a revocation of the repudiation. This he can do whether she be willing or not.'[53]

Obedience, Maintenance, and Beating

- Obedience is considered a duty of the wife. A wife should be obedient to her husband insofar as his commands are legally allowed and are ordained as duties of marriage. If a wife is disobedient, she loses her right to maintenance. According to Hanafi jurisprudence, a wife is considered disobedient if she leaves their home without the consent of her husband or without a lawful excuse. Other schools of jurisprudence, however, say that even if she stays at home, she will not be entitled to maintenance if she refuses sexual intercourse.[54] A husband may beat his wife if she is disobedient. The husband can resort to several measures when his wife disobeys him, the last of which is the most severe: beating her. If the woman obeys him, then he should stop using these measures.[55]

Maintenance after Divorce

- Maintenance for a divorced wife ceases after the *iddah* period, the three-month waiting period after the divorce.
- After a divorce, the wife is only entitled to the sum of money set in the marriage contract: the *muakhar*.

Inheritance

- A Muslim woman receives less than the share of a Muslim man when both parties have an equal degree of relationship to the deceased person. Hence, a sister inherits from her father half of what her brother inherits. A Muslim husband inherits half of what his wife leaves, provided that she did not have a son. If she does, then the husband inherits a quarter. A Muslim wife inherits a quarter of her husband's estate if he has no son. If he has a son, then she inherits an eighth.[56]

- Being of a different religion is a total bar to inheritance. Thus a Muslim may neither inherit from, nor leave an inheritance to, a non-Muslim.[57]

Custody of Children

- After a divorce, the custody of a child is entrusted to either the mother or father, depending on the child's age and sex. Younger children tend to be placed in the mother's care and the father takes over custody when the child reaches a given age. However, shari'a makes a distinction between custody and guardianship: the father is the guardian of the child after separation even if the mother is granted the right to custody up to a certain age, after which custody reverts to the father.[58]
- If the mother decides to remarry she automatically loses her right to custody.

Testimony

The testimony of two women equals that of one man. Originally this rule was meant for financial affairs; but the jurists expanded the rule and made it a general rule.

* * *

This overview leads us to the question: What type of Islamic law is being implemented within Britain's shari'a courts? The short answer is: the classical Islamic law with all its contradictions and discrimination.

From their perspective, what they are applying is not only *fiqh*, the jurists' traditions. They are applying what they think of literally as God's law, the law of Allah. Hence, depending on the type of shari'a court applying this law, it can either seek a fundamentalist interpretation of *fiqh*, or it can try to make the lives of women easier by seeking the most lenient interpretation. But the mindset is framed by the perception that shari'a is God's law and therefore better than any other secular law. The mindset is also shaped by the acceptance of the rules I mentioned above, that regulate marriage, divorce, polygamy, guardianship, inheritance, etc., anything related to family affairs and women's position within the family. They accept these rules and do not question them. Hence during my interviews with five 'judges', including a female member of a Shari'a council, they reflected their perception that this *is what Islam commands, this is what God commands, and we are following God's law.*

Within this mindset, the jurists' traditions somehow seem to become sacred in these judges' minds; they reflect a 'divine wisdom' that transcends our understanding. Naturally this leads them to apply the classical Islamic law to the letter, picking and choosing as they want from within that pool of traditions.

Consider the issue of the proper age for marriage. Sheikh Siddiqi of the Muslim Arbitration Tribunal is clear regarding this issue.

> Sheikh Siddiqi: In my view, puberty is the right age. But puberty is the minimum age; then the next criterion is the decision of the guardian, he has to make the decision. Because in some societies, 12- or 13-year-old women, girls, they are more or less fully fledged women, they are fully functional, and you in Western societies, [...] are having babies, they are having sex, so they are fully grown and fully mature; there are some 12-year-olds that are not in that condition, they are very weak, they are not fully functional as women, and they do not want to get married. So it is the job of the *wali*, the guardian, to ensure that the girl is protected and the girl is not subjected to a marriage in this situation where her personal circumstances do not allow this marriage to take place.

Again, we see classical Islamic jurisprudence being used as a point of reference in these courts.

The guardianship issue clearly illustrates this point. As we saw above, Sheikh Siddiqi considers that the guardian knows best for his ward. Dr Mohammad Shahoot Kharfan, of the Muslim Welfare House, demands that the bride and the groom and the guardian be present at the wedding ceremony. But to contract the marriage, the guardian has to approve. One example he gave me was of a woman in her thirties who wanted to marry. Dr Kharfan asked for her guardian to contract the marriage. When she told him he lives in another country, he called him to get his approval and to ask him to delegate his right of guardianship to another person, a male of course. When I asked Dr Kharfan if her voice was not enough, his answer was matter-of-fact: 'the guardian is present, the guardian is present', meaning, we have a guardian here, and he will decide.

By the same token, Hanafi jurisprudence allows the guardian to annul the marriage of his female ward if he is not satisfied with her choice of the groom, and the people I interviewed consider this provision valid. In fact, it has been used and applied in the Islamic Shari'a Council, Leyton, and the Birmingham Islamic Shari'a Council of the Central Mosque. As I said before, the latter is considered to be supportive of women's needs.

Conclusion

Context matters. Looking at the context of women's reality allows us to understand why women are turning to shari'a councils in the UK in the first place. They go to them because they want a *religious divorce*. They are not seeking mediation. What they need is a religious divorce. Unlike what many claim, women can satisfy this demand within the British legal system; they do not need the shari'a courts.

And so do *consequences. They too matter.* Again, and I will not tire of repeating this: The moment the state starts to situate rights within a group rights frame rather than an individual frame, the outcome will likely be segregation, inequality, and discrimination. The weakest will be left vulnerable, subject to abuse and discrimination. This is the main consequence of legal pluralism in its two forms: weak and strong.

A key consequence of introducing weak legal pluralism and with it Islamic law in Western legal systems will be a stratified citizenry, involving two types of women: Western women who can enjoy their rights based on the state's laws, and migrant women who cannot. The system in the UK has in effect created these two types of citizens: one enjoys equality before the law and the other does not because of their religious identity. These women suffer from the *double discrimination syndrome*: in addition to gender discrimination they are also denied access to their legal rights. Indeed, this stratification will only further cement the walls around the closed parallel societies.

In addition, the system is, de facto, legitimising polygamous marriages, and facilitating child marriage and forced marriage. Most significantly for the cohesion and unity of society and the fight against extremism, it has continued to separate minority groups from their wider society and has given Islamists a free hand in reinforcing their social control over closed communities.

Throughout this chapter I have taken a position that defends the universality of human rights. Using the words of Frank La Rue, the former UN Special Rapporteur on the Promotion and Protection of the Right to Freedom of Opinion and Expression, these universal human rights are simply the 'minimum standards for protection'[59] for every person in any society. They are the minimum that one should expect in any society. The struggles of men and women fighting for these universal rights in different societies of the globe testify to this fact.

I argue therefore that special treatments for specific groups and the introduction of religious laws will only undermine this very universality and the protection granted by the international standards of human rights. I maintain that, rather than deliberating about whether human rights are universal or culturally determined, we should use a consequence-based approach to add needed substance to the discussion. We must bring in the human face of the suffering that results when human rights are violated – whether those are the rights of individuals or a larger society.

Such an approach can illuminate the grave consequences of violating human rights and make the case that doing so is by nature *bad*. Once we establish this fact, we will dare to make the moral judgment that these violations are *wrong*. It will also help us turn the discussion around. Rather than making frantic efforts to answer the question of whether human rights are universal, the question will be: why are these rights being violated in the first place?[60]

A consequence-based approach to human rights reflects the idea that from a moral point of view what is most important is to 'consider how one's actions are likely to affect others'. After all, 'It is the consequences of one's actions, not the intentions behind them, which form the most relevant benchmark for measuring the moral worth of an action.'[61] If we are to apply this approach in concrete steps to our subject matter, we should look at the consequences on two levels. On the *individual* level, what individual harm is being done to the girl or woman through the application of a parallel legal system (shari'a law)? And on the *societal* level, what are the general negative consequences for society of segregating groups and creating what Amartya Sen called the monoculturalism of closed communities?

Once we understand the consequences of the parallel religious legal orders in the UK and of efforts to introduce group and identity politics and policies based on difference, we see the need for specific policy recommendations.

Policy Recommendations

British Muslim women do not need saving. They need solutions. A system that leaves the most vulnerable subject to abuse and discrimination is not a fair system. This is the system we see today in Britain and the state is yet to fulfil its obligation to protect the most vulnerable in society. The latest report of CIVITAS written by Emma Webb has highlighted the urgent need for action. It argued that 'while there is no silver bullet, there are legal and policy solutions to individual challenges that aggravate the situation ... and can protect individuals from discrimination and abuse within their communities'.[62]

I suggest that the UK government consider six policy recommendations to address the problems that women endure when they turn to shari'a courts within the framework of the UK legal system. These recommendations are also very important and relevant to other European and North American countries.

1 Amend current legislation to make mandatory the registration of all religious marriages in the UK, in line with the proposals of the Marriage Act 1949 (Amendment) Bill.[63]

2 Launch a nationwide campaign to register all Islamic marriages. This will ultimately reveal many polygamous marriages. The women who are parties to these marriages, and their children, should be protected. But that protection should not entail recognising polygamy as a form of marriage.

3 Be consequent in the application of laws prohibiting polygamy/ bigamy.

4 Attach to the British court system a unit (with local branches nationwide) that are authorised to automatically issues an Islamic divorce after the civil divorce has been issued: a decree absolute. In many Islamic countries, the religious authorities recognise a civil divorce as religiously valid; the situation should be the same in the UK.

5 Launch a nationwide campaign that reaches women within closed communities to inform them about their rights, the importance and protection of civil marriage, the need to register their marriage, and how the law functions in the UK.

6 Abolish the parallel religious legal systems in the UK, and treat citizens and migrants as equal before the law.

Notes

1 Gordon Woodman, "The Idea of Legal Pluralism", in Baudoiun Dupret, Maurits Berger and Laila al-Zawini (eds), *Legal Pluralism in the Arab World*, (The Hague: Kluwer Law International, 1999), p. 4.

2 Prakash Shah, *Legal Pluralism in Conflict: Coping with Cultural Diversity in Law*, (London: Glasshouse Press, 2005), p. ix.

3 Denis MacEoin, "Shari'a Law Or 'One Law for All'?", David G. Green (ed.), Sharia Law or 'One Law for All'? *Institute for the Study of Civil Society*, (London: CIVITAS, 2009), pp. 9–127; John Rawls, *A Theory of*

Justice, Revised Edition, (Cambridge, Massachusetts: Belknap Press of Harvard University Press, 2005); Ronald Dworkin, *Law's Empire*, (Cambridge, MA: Belknap Press of Harvard University Press, 1986); Ihsan Yilmaz, *Muslim Laws, Politics and Society in Modern Nations States: Dynamic Legal Pluralism in England, Turkey and Pakistan*, (England: Ashgate Publishing Limited, 2005); Werner Menski, *Comparative Law in a Global Context: The Legal Systems of Asia and Africa*, Second Edition, (Cambridge: Cambridge University Press, 2006); Dupret, Berger and al-Zawini (eds), *Legal Pluralism in the Arab World*; Michael Kemper und Maurus Reinkowski (Hg.), *Rechtspluralismus in der islamischen Welt: Gewohnheitsrecht zwischen Staat und Gesellschaft*, (Berlin: Walter de Gruyter, 2005).

4   For more information on this discourse please see Wolfgang Kashuba, "Wie Fremde gemacht werden", *Der Tagesspiegel*, (14 January 2007), <http://www.tagesspiegel.de/meinung/kommentare/wie-fremde-gemacht-werden/798460.html>, accessed 20 April 2010; Wolfgang Kaschuba, "Ethnische Parallelgesllschaften?: Zur kulturellen Konstruktion des Fremden in der europäischen Migration", *Zeitschrift für Volkskunde* 1 (2007), pp. 65–85; Bernhard Heininger, *Ehrenmord und Emanzipation: Die Geschlechterfrage in Ritualen von Parallelgesellschaften*, (Berlin: LIT Verlag, 2009); Werner Schiffauer, *Parallelgesellschaften*, (Bielefeld: transcript Verlag, 2008).

5   Colin Brown, "Let Us Adopt Islamic Family Law to Curb Extremists, Muslims Tell Kelly", *The Independent*, (15 August 2006), available at <http://www.independent.co.uk/news/uk/politics/let-us-adopt-islamic-family-law-to-curb-extremists-muslims-tell-kelly-411954.html>, accessed 15 July 2015.

6   Ihsan Yilmaz, *Muslim Laws, Politics and Society in Modern Nation States: Dynamic Legal Pluralism in England, Turkey and Pakistan*, (Surrey: Ashgate Publishing, 2005), p. 2.

7   See Ralph Grillo,Roger Ballard, Alessandro Ferrari, André J. Hoekema, Marcel Maussen and Prakash Shah(eds), *Legal Practice and Cultural Diversity*, (Surrey: Ashgate, 2009); John Griffiths, "What Is Legal Pluralism?" The Journal of Legal Pluralism and Unofficial Law, 18(24) (1986), pp. 1–55; Ihsan Yilmaz, "The Challenge of Post-Modern Legality and Muslim Legal Pluralism in England", *Journal of Ethnic and Migration Studies*, 28 (2) (April 2002), pp. 343–354; Yilmaz, *Muslim Laws*; Dupret, Berger and al-Zwaini (eds), *Legal Pluralism in the Arab World*; Kemper and Reinkowski (eds), *Rechtspluralismus in der islamischen Welt*.

8   Grillo et al. (eds), pp. 25–26.

9   Jack Donnelly, "Cultural Relativism and Universal Human Rights", *Human Rights Quarterly* vi(4) (November 1984), p. 401.

10   Ibid.

11   For more information on the actual experience with legal pluralism in non-Western countries see chapter three in Elham Manea, *Women and Shari'a Law: The Impact of Legal Pluralism in the UK*, (London: I.B., Tauris, 2016), pp. 54–89.

12   Lorenzo Divino, *The New Muslim Brotherhood in the West*, (New York: Columbia University Press, 2010), p. 115; Office for National Statistics

(ONS), "FOI Request: Statistics of the Muslim Population in the UK for 2011, 2012, 2013", (London: ONS, 16 May 2013).

13 N. N., "Europe's Growing Muslim Population", (29 November 2017), Pew Research Center, <http://www.pewforum.org/2017/11/29/europes-growing-muslim-population/>.

14 For more information on the work of Shari'a Councils, see Samia Bono, *Muslim Women and Shari'ah Councils: Transcending the Boundaries of Community and Law*, (London: Palgrave Macmillan, 2012).

15 See Manea, *Women and Sharia Law*, 2016.

16 Salma Dean, interview by author, London: House of Lords, (9 August 2013); Charlotte Proudman, interview by author, London, (17 January 2013).

17 Bano, *Muslim Women and Shari'ah Councils*, p. 186; Sonia Nurin Shah-Kazemi, "Untying the Knot: Muslim Women, Divorce and the Shariah", *Nuffield Foundation*, (London: Nuffield Foundation, 2001), p. 48.

18 Charlotte Proudman, interview, January 2013.

19 "The Truth about Islamic Marriage", Channel 4, 18:00; "New Channel 4 Survey Reveals the Truth about Muslim Marriage", Channel 4, (20 November 2017), available at <https://www.channel4.com/press/news/new-channel-4-survey-reveals-truth-aboutmuslim-marriage>. The Survey's

> Data were tabulated by ICM analysed from the responses of 923 participants from 14 cities across Britain – Glasgow, Newcastle, Preston, Bradford, Stockport, Manchester, Stoke on Trent, Leicester, Birmingham, Oxford, Cardiff, London, Bristol, Gloucester and Cambridge. The survey targeted women who had been married in the UK. In terms of age and ethnicity, the sample reflects what is known about the British Muslim population.

20 Emma Webb, "Fallen through the Cracks: Unregistered Islamic Marriages in England and Wales, and the Future of Legislative Reform", *Institute for the Study of Civil Society*, (London: Civitas, August 2020), p. 5, available at <https://civitas.org.uk/publications/fallen-through-the-cracks/>, accessed 25 August 2020.

21 Cassandra Balchin, "Registering Muslim Marriages", (London: *Critical Muslim* website, 2011), available at <http://criticalmuslim.com/upfront/religion/registering-muslim-marriages-cassandra-balchin>, accessed 9 July 2015.

22 Field work in the UK in January and August 2013. See also Balchin, "Registering Muslim Marriages"; Divya Talwa, "Wedding Trouble as UK Muslim Marriages Not Recognised", *BBC News*, (3 February 2010), available at <http://news.bbc.co.uk/2/hi/uk_news/8493660.stm> accessed 9 July 2015.

23 Shah-Kazemi, "Untying the Knot", p. 31.

24 Bano, *Muslim Women and Shari'ah Councils*, pp. 160–161.

25 Talwa, "Wedding Trouble"; on polygamous marriages in the UK also see Linda Serck, "Polygamy in Islam: The Women Victims of Multiple Marriage", *BBC News*, (1 June 2012), available at <http://www.bbc.com/news/uk-england-berkshire-18252958>, accessed 9 July 2015.

26   Balchin, "Registering Muslim Marriages".
27   Sister Sabah, interview by author, 23 January 2013.
28   Birmingham Mosque Trust (BMT), "Islamic Divorce (Khula) Procedure", (Birmingham: Birmingham Mosque Trust, 2015), available at <http://centralmosque.org.uk/downloads/62_Islamic%20Divorce-Procedure.pdf>, accessed 9 July 2015.
29   Sheikh Mohammad Talha Bokhari, interview by author, Birmingham, (23 January 2013).
30   Dr Mohammad Shahoot Kharfan, interview by author, London, (22 January 2013).
31   Salim Leham, interview by author, London, (18 January 2013).
32   Sheikh Dr Suhaib Hasan, interview by author, London, (28 January 2013).
33   Bano, *Muslim Women and Shari'ah Councils*, p. 186; Shah-Kazemi, "Untying the Knot", p. 34.
34   Shah-Kazemi, "Untying the Knot", p. 35.
35   Bano, *Muslim Women and Shari'ah Councils*, pp. 210–212.
36   Ibid., p. 213.
37   Ibid.
38   Charlotte Rachael Proudman, *Equal and Free? Evidence in Support of Baroness Cox's Arbitration and Mediation Services (Equality) Bill*, (London: House of Lords, May 2012), pp. 11–39.
39   Quoted in Ibid., p. 33.
40   Quoted in Ibid., p. 29.
41   Haitham al-Haddad, "Fatwa: A Civil Divorce Is Not a Valid Religious Divorce", *Islam21c.com*, (21 July 2010), available at <http://www.islam21c.com/fataawa/912-fatwa-a-civil-divorce-is-not-a-valid-islamic-divorce/>, accessed 9 July 2015.
42   Sohail Akbar Warraich and Cassandra Balchin, "Recognizing the Un-recognized: Inter-country Cases and Muslim Marriages & Divorces in Britain", *Women Living Under Muslim Laws*, (London: Women Living Under Muslim Laws, 2006), p. 3.
43   Rashad Ali, "Islam, 'Shari'ah Courts, Islamisation and the Far-Right'", *Democratiya* 16 (Spring/Summer 2009), pp. 47–48. It is worth mentioning that even the European Council for Fatwa and Research (ECFR) – an affiliate of the global Muslim Brothers – reluctantly issued a religious decision acknowledging the validity of a divorce issued by a non-Muslim. ECFR, Fifth Regular Session, (4–7 May, Dublin, 2000). Available at <http://goo.gl/hGOAeK>, accessed 9 July 2015.
44   Sheikh Mohammad Talha Bokhari, interview by author, Birmingham, (23 January 2013).
45   Majid Khadduri, "Human Rights in Islam", *Annals of the American Academy of Political and Social Science* 243 (January 1946), p. 79.
46   'Abdallāh Aḥmad An-Na'im, *Toward an Islamic Reformation : Civil Liberties, Human Rights, and International Law*, (Syracuse, NY: Syracuse University Press, 2005), p. 171.
47   Ahmed Shukri, *Muhammedan Law of Marriage and Divorce*, (New York: Ams Press, 1996), p. 21.
48   Ibid.

49 Yemen's Family Law No. 20, 1992 states in Article 1: 'Marriage is a union between the couple by a legal charter; it gives the man legal permission to access the woman (sexually), and together they establish a family based on good companionship'. Kuwaiti Personal Status Law, No. 51, 1984, states in Article 1: 'Marriage is a contract between a man and a woman. [With it] a woman becomes legally (sexually) accessible to the man; and its aim is settlement, chastity, and the strength of the nation.' The Syrian Islamic Personal Status Law, No. 59, 1953, says in Article 1: 'Marriage is a contract between a man and a woman. [With it] a woman becomes legally accessible to the man (sexually); and its aim is building a mutual life bond and children.' This perception of marriage does change, however, when the Islamic law is reformed as with the case of the reformed Moroccan Family Code (*Moudawana*) of 2004, which states in Article 4 that

> Marriage is a legal contract by which a man and a woman mutually consent to unite in a common and enduring conjugal life. Its purpose is fidelity, virtue and the creation of a stable family, under the supervision of both spouses according to the provisions of this Moudawana.

50 For more on this subject see Andrea Büchler and Christina Schlatter, "Marriage Age in Islamic and Contemporary Muslim Family Laws: A Comparative Survey", *Electronic Journal of Islamic and Middle Eastern Law* 1 (2013), pp. 37–74.

51 Elham Manea, *Ich will nicht mehr schweigen: Der Islam, der Westen und die Menschenrechte* (Freiburg: Herder Verlag, 2009), p. 34.

52 Some of the Twelver Shi'a jurists added the condition that for a woman to enjoy this right, she should previously have been married. For more details on the jurisprudences positions on guardianship see Wael B. Hallaq, *Shari'a: Theory, Practice and Transformations*, (Cambridge: Cambridge University Press, 2007), pp. 274–276.

53 Ahmed Shukri, *Muhammedan Law of Marriage and Divorce*, p. 97.

54 Ibid., p. 81; David Pearl, *A Textbook on Muslim Law*, (London: Croom Helm, 1979), p. 65.

55 Manea, *Ich will nicht mehr schweigen*, pp. 141–143.

56 Imam Mohammad Abu Zahrah, *Ahkam Al Tirkat wa al Mawari'ith - Provisions for Legacies and Inheritances*, in Arabic, (Beirut: Dar Al Fikr Al Arabi, 1963), pp. 122, 131; An-Na'im, "Toward an Islamic Reformation", p. 176.

57 An-Na'im, Ibid., p. 176.

58 Chibli Mallat, *Introduction to Middle Eastern Law*, (Oxford: Oxford University Press, 2007), p. 357.

59 Frank La Rue, discussion with author by Skype, (23 July 2015).

60 Elham Manea, "Islam and Human Dignity: A Consequence-Based Approach to Human Dignity and Rights", in Dorothèe Deimann and Simon Mugier (eds), *Entgegensprechen: Texte zu Menschenwürde und Menschenrecht*, vol. 1, (Basel: Edition Gesowip, 2010), p. 520.

61 Brian Orend, *Human Rights: Concept and Context*, (Peterborough: Broadview Press, 2002), p. 89, quoted in Manea, ibid., pp. 513–514.

62 Webb, op. cit., p. 111.

63 Ibid., p. 112.

Bibliography

Books

Abu Zahrah, Imam Mohammad, *Ahkam Al Tirkat wa al Mawari'ith - Provisions for Legacies and Inheritances,* in Arabic, (Beirut: Dar Al Fikr Al Arabi, 1963).

An-Na'im, Abdullahi Ahmed, *Toward Islamic Reformation: Civil Liberties, Human Rights, and International Law,* (Syracuse, NY: Syracuse University Press, 1990).

Bono, Samia, *Muslim Women and Shari'ah Councils: Transcending the Boundaries of Community and Law,* (London: Palgrave Macmillan, 2012).

Divino, Lorenzo, *The New Muslim Brotherhood in the West,* (New York: Columbia University Press, 2010).

Dupret, Baudoiun, Berger, Maurits and al-Zawini, Laila (eds), *Legal Pluralism in the Arab World,* (The Hague: Kluwer Law International, 1999).

Dworkin, Ronald, *Law's Empire,* (Cambridge, MA: Belknap Press of Harvard University Press, 1986).

Grillo, Ralph, Roger Ballard, Alessandro Ferrari, André J. Hoekema, Marcel Maussen and Prakash Shah (eds), *Legal Practice and Cultural Diversity,* (Surrey: Ashgate, 2009).

Hallaq, Wael B. *Shari'a: Theory, Practice and Transformations,* (Cambridge: Cambridge University Press, 2007).

Heininger, Bernhard, *Ehrenmord und Emanzipation: Die Geschlechterfrage in Ritualen von Parallelgesellschaften,* (Berlin: LIT Verlag, 2009); Schiffauer, Werner, *Parallelgesellschaften,* (Bielefeld: Transcript Verlag, 2008).

Kemper, Michael und Reinkowski, Maurus (Hg.), *Rechtspluralismus in der islamischen Welt: Gewohnheitsrecht zwischen Staat und Gesellschaft,* (Berlin: Walter de Gruyter, 2005).

Mallat, Chibli, *Introduction to Middle Eastern Law,* (Oxford: Oxford University Press, 2007).

Manea, Elham, *Ich will nicht mehr schweigen: Der Islam, der Westen und die Menschenrechte,* (Freiburg: Herder Verlag, 2009).

Manea, Elham, *Women and Shari'a Law: The Impact of Legal Pluralism in the UK,* (London: I.B. Tauris, 2016).

Menski, Werner, *Comparative Law in a Global Context: The Legal Systems of Asia and Africa,* Second Edition, (Cambridge: Cambridge University Press, 2006).

Pearl, David, *A Textbook on Muslim Law,* (London: Croom Helm, 1979).

Rawls, John, *A Theory of Justice,* Revised Edition, (Cambridge, MA: Belknap Press of Harvard University Press, 2005).

Shah, Prakash, *Legal Pluralism in Conflict: Coping with Cultural Diversity in Law,* (London: Glasshouse Press, 2005).

Shukri, Ahmed, *Muhammedan Law of Marriage and Divorce,* (New York: Ams Press, 1996).

Yilmaz, Ihsan, *Muslim Laws, Politics and Society in Modern Nations States: Dynamic Legal Pluralism in England, Turkey and Pakistan,* (Oxford: Ashgate Publishing Limited, 2005).

Periodicals

Ali, Rashad, "Islam, 'Shari'ah Courts, Islamisation and the Far-Right'", *Democratiya* 16 (Spring/Summer 2009), pp. 45–52.

Büchler, Andrea and Schlatter, Christina, "Marriage Age in Islamic and Contemporary Muslim Family Laws: A Comparative Survey", *Electronic Journal of Islamic and Middle Eastern Law* 1 (2013), pp. 37–74.

Donnelly, Jack, "Cultural Relativism and Universal Human Rights", *Human Rights Quarterly* vi(4) (November 1984), pp. 400–419

Griffiths, John, "What Is Legal Pluralism?", *Journal of Legal Pluralism* 32(24) (1986), pp. 1–55.

Kaschuba, Wolfgang, "Ethnische Parallelgesllschaften: Zur kulturellen Konstruktion des Fremden in der europäischen Migration", *Zeitschrift für Volkskunde* 1 (2007), pp. 65–85.

Khadduri, Majid, "Human Rights in Islam", *Annals of the American Academy of Political and Social Science* 243 (January 1946), pp. 77–81.

MacEoin, Denis, "Shari'a Law Or 'One Law for All'?", *Institute for the Study of Civil Society*, (London: CIVITAS, 2009).

Yilmaz, Ihsan, 'The Challenge of Post-Modern Legality and Muslim Legal Pluralism in England', *Journal of Ethnic and Migration Studies* xxvii(2) (April 2002), pp. 343–354.

Articles

Brown, Colin, 'Let Us Adopt Islamic Family Law to Curb Extremists, Muslims Tell Kelly', *The Independent*, (15 August 2006), available at <http://www.independent.co.uk/news/uk/politics/let-us-adopt-islamic-family-law-to-curb-extremists-muslims-tell-kelly-411954.html>.

Kashuba, Wolfgang, "Wie Fremde gemacht werden", *Der Tagesspiegel*, (14 January 2007), http://www.tagesspiegel.de/meinung/kommentare/wie-fremde-gemacht-werden/798460.html>.

Talwa, Divya, 'Wedding Trouble as UK Muslim Marriages Not Recognised', *BBC News*, (3 February 2010), available at <http://news.bbc.co.uk/2/hi/uk_news/8493660.stm>.

Serck, Linda 'Polygamy in Islam: The Women Victims of Multiple Marriage', *BBC News*, (1 June 2012), available at <http://www.bbc.com/news/uk-england-berkshire-18252958>.

Chapters, Documentaries, Reports, Statistics and Websites

Al-Haddad, Haitham, "Fatwa: A Civil Divorce Is Not a Valid Religious Divorce", *Islam21c.com*, (21 July 2010), available at <http://www.islam21c.com/fataawa/912-fatwa-a-civil-divorce-is-not-a-valid-islamic-divorce/>.

Balchin, Cassandra, "Registering Muslim Marriages", (London: *Critical Muslim* website, 2011), available at <http://criticalmuslim.com/upfront/religion/registering-muslim-marriages-cassandra-balchin>.

Birmingham Mosque Trust (BMT), "Islamic Divorce (Khula) Procedure", (Birmingham: Birmingham Mosque Trust, 2015), available at <http://centralmosque.org.uk/downloads/62_Islamic%20Divorce-Procedure.pdf>.

Proudman, Rachael Charlotte, *Equal and Free? Evidence in Support of Baroness Cox's Arbitration and Mediation Services (Equality) Bill*, (London: House of Lords, May 2012).

N. N., "Europe's Growing Muslim Population", *Pew Research Center*, (29 November 2017), http://www.pewforum.org/2017/11/29/europes-growing-muslim-population/.

Manea, Elham, "Islam and Human Dignity: A Consequence-Based Approach to Human Dignity and Rights", in Dorothèe Deimann and Simon Mugier (eds), *Entgegensprechen: Texte zu Menschenwürde und Menschenrecht*, vol. 1 (Basel: Edition Gesowip, 2010), p. 520.

Office for National Statistics (ONS), "FOI Request: Statistics of the Muslim Population in the UK for 2011, 2012, 2013", (London: ONS, 16 May 2013).

Sonia Nurin Shah-Kazemi, "Untying the Knot: Muslim Women, Divorce and the Shariah", *Nuffield Foundation*, (London: Nuffield Foundation, 2001).

"The Truth about Islamic Marriage", Channel 4, 18:00; "New Channel 4 Survey Reveals the Truth about Muslim Marriage", Channel 4, (20 November 2017), available at: <https://www.channel4.com/press/news/new-channel-4-survey-reveals-truth-aboutmuslim-marriage>.

Warraich, Sohail Akbar and Balchin, Cassandra, "Recognizing the Unrecognized: Inter-country Cases and Muslim Marriages & Divorces in Britain", *Women Living Under Muslim Laws*, (London: Women Living Under Muslim Laws, 2006).

Webb, Emma, "Fallen through the Cracks: Unregistered Islamic Marriages in England and Wales, and the Future of Legislative Reform", *Institute for the Study of Civil Society*, (London: Civitas, August 2020), available at <https://civitas.org.uk/publications/fallen-through-the-cracks/>.

Laws

Moroccan Family Code (*Moudawana*) of 2004.
Yemen's Family Law No. 20, 1992.

Cited Interviews

Bokhari, Sheikh Mohammad Talha (Coordinator of the Islamic shari'a Council in Birmingham and one of its members), Birmingham, (23 January 2013).

Charlotte, Proudman (Human Rights Barrister), London, (17 January 2013).

Dean, Salma (Human Rights Barrister worked on Baroness Cox's team on the Equality Bill), interview by author, London: House of Lords, (9 August 2013).

Hasan, Sheikh Dr Suhaib (the Islamic Shari'a Council in Leyton), Leyton, (28 January 2013).

Kharfan, Dr Mohammad Shahoot (Imam at Muslim Welfare House East London), London, (22 January 2013).

La Rue, Frank (Former UN Special Rapporteur on the Promotion and Protection of the Right to Freedom of Opinion and Expression), Skype interview, (23 July 2015).

Leham, Salim (Legal Director of the Muslim Welfare House in East London), London, (18 January 2013).

Siddiqi, Sheikh Faizul Aqtab (the Director of the Muslim Arbitration Council), Nuneaton, (15 January 2013).

Sister Sabah (Administrative Coordinator of the Family Support Service at the Islamic shari'a Council in Birmingham), Birmingham (23 January 2013).

3 Shariah Councils in the UK
Reform and Regulation

Dr Islam Uddin

Introduction

This chapter examines the practices of Shariah councils in the UK. Shariah Councils are quasi-legal, unofficial bodies that function to mediate, arbitrate and issue Muslim divorce certificates.[1] There is an ongoing debate for and against the use of Shariah Councils in Britain. Those opposed to Shariah Councils argue that English law is best suited to protect women and that Shariah Councils are operating as a parallel legal system and acting as courts.[2] Whereas those opposing such views argue that Shariah Councils know their legal limits and operate within the law as legitimate mechanisms of alternative dispute resolution.[3] Some raise concerns that an increase in unregistered marriages among British Muslims[4] and the lack of awareness regarding the availability of legal aid in civil divorce cases[5] cause Muslim women to use Shariah Councils for dispute resolution. Shariah Councils are criticised for following interpretations of Islamic norms and values, which marginalise women and provide favourable terms for men.[6] Others assert Shariah Councils discriminate against Muslim women who are coerced into using them and concede their civil rights.[7] Malik contends that there are considerable empirical gaps in understanding the experience of those who use a non-state normative field of social action and whether they face unjust outcomes or secure autonomy as individuals.[8]

In 2016, the government launched an independent review to explore whether Sharia law was incompatible with the laws of England and Wales.[9] The findings of the review were published in 2018 and it made recommendations in three areas: the amendment of the Marriage Act 1949 to make compulsory the registration of Muslim marriage, an awareness campaign for women's right under civil law and the regulation of Shariah Councils.[10] In response to the report, the government said it would consider the review's finding, but ruled out

DOI: 10.4324/9781003090410-4

the proposal of state-regulating Shariah Councils to avoid conferring legitimacy as an alternative form of dispute resolution.[11]

In light of such debates, this chapter presents the findings of an empirical study on marriage and divorce among British Muslims which includes an examination of Shariah Councils. The chapter starts with a background of Muslims in Britain, an overview of the problems associated with marriage and divorce, and explains the research methodology. The chapter then presents the findings concerning marriage, divorce and Shariah Councils; and concludes with recommendations for the reform and regulation of Shariah Councils.

Background

According to the last census in 2011, the Muslim population in Britain is 2.7 million, making Islam the second-largest religion in the UK, with the majority of Muslims having origins in South Asia, in countries such as Pakistan, Bangladesh and India.[12] These migrant communities in Britain strived to maintain elements of family life from their countries of origin, giving them a distinct ethnoreligious identity.[13] In particular, Muslim family life represents one of the greatest expressions of religious identity; and therefore, Muslims may increasingly feel a need for religious marriage (*nikah*) and divorce (*talaq*).[14] Hence, many Muslims will marry and divorce according to the customary laws of their country of origin.[15]

In English law legislation such as the Marriage Act 1949 and Matrimonial Causes Act 1973 stipulates the conditions for a legally binding marriage and divorce. *Nikah* ceremonies conducted in the UK must comply with the Marriage Act to form a legally valid marriage, i.e. take place in a building registered for the solemnisation of marriages and in the presence of a registrar or an authorised person. *Nikah* ceremonies that do not comply with the Marriage Act are considered 'non-marriages'; the couple are treated as cohabitees and do not have the same rights and protections as a married couple, and civil courts do not have the same powers to make financial orders as to when to grant a divorce for the dissolution of a valid marriage.[16] Hence, the concern is that *nikah*-only marriages leave Muslim women with little security and rights, vulnerable to exploitation within the marriage[17]and Muslim women who rely on Shariah Councils may face unfavourable terms when negotiating an Islamic divorce.[18] Others call for an amendment to the law to ensure services offered by imams and Shariah Councils fall within the Marriage Act 1949 and the Equality Act 2010.[19] The Independent Review acknowledged the difficulty in obtaining first-hand accounts of negative experiences of using Shariah Councils[20]; thus the need for further research to substantiate such claims.

The research referenced in this chapter involved in-depth interviews with British Muslim women and interviews with professionals (i.e. experts) ranging from Shariah Council judges, imams, to solicitors and counsellors, identified as providing services to Muslim women during the marriage, marital disputes and divorce. Shariah Council hearings were observed and their procedural documents analysed. The findings provide a valuable insight into the practice of marriage and divorce among British Muslims and the experience of Shariah Councils. To maintain anonymity, the participants' identifications have been removed from the data collected and pseudonyms used to replace their real names in reporting the findings.

Marriage

The majority of the participants had a civil registered marriage. However, one of the main considerations to emerge from the findings was the importance of *nikah* in validating their marriage as explained by the participants.

> The civil marriage to me is just a paper, so for me, it's all about the *nikah*.
>
> (Henna)

> I thought it was strange that he would not give me the Islamic divorce because I believed in Islamic marriage more than the court marriage [i.e. civil marriage].
>
> (Fahima)

Nikah literally means 'to tie up together' and in Muslim family law refers to the marriage contract, providing a social and legal relationship for founding a family.[21] *Nikah* is seen as a moral imperative and binding contract,[22] one that allows Muslim couple to cohabit and not violate community norms.[23] The imams and solicitors in this study agreed that *nikah* was a necessity for Muslims.

> Obviously, any Muslim has to get an Islamic marriage, it's a norm. I mean a Muslim cannot be married until they do the Islamic *nikah*.
>
> (Imam #1)

Clients have a religious need for a *nikah* ceremony. The family accept the *nikah*.

(Solicitor #1)

Therefore, any consideration for a civil marriage was a secondary issue as it did not constitute the actual marriage. The Shariah Council judges explained why a civil marriage was not sufficient from a religious perspective, which related to the conditions of the Muslim marriage contract and the perception of civil marriage among the Muslim community.

There are four conditions of an Islamic marriage: 1) offer and acceptance, 2) two witnesses, 3) *wali amr* (guardian) and 4) *mahr* (dower). In a civil registration, the first two points are present and the last two are absent.

(SC Judge #3)

Civil registration is for legal convenience i.e. benefits and taxes. For Muslims, the civil registry is not getting married but a pre-party to the *nikah*, it carries no weight. The *nikah* has weight in the eyes of God, faith and the community. The couple would not live together after civil registration.

(SC Judge #1)

Empirical studies from other diasporic Muslim communities worldwide show similar findings whereby the *nikah* is sufficient for the Muslim community seen as the "real" marriage[24]; Akhtar found British Muslims do not register their marriages as there are no incentives for a civil ceremony, which added no further value to the status of being married in their perceptions.[25] Nevertheless, the Shariah Council still required a copy of the civil marriage certificate before they could provide the original *nikah-nama* (Muslim marriage contract); until then, they only provide a photocopy. Whereas the Shariah Council required non-EU nationals to have a civil marriage first even before applying for a *nikah* ceremony. The Shariah Council explained why they ask for proof of a civil marriage.

We ask for a copy of the civil registration, to avoid fake marriages and temporary marriages, we insist couples show real commitment before the original *nikah* certificate is issued.

(SC Judge #1)

The status of civil marriage is important in *nikah* applications with the Shariah Council, though they do not consider a civil ceremony as an Islamic marriage. Furthermore, by insisting on a civil registration certificate, the Shariah Council was able to avoid conducting polygamous marriages for legal and moral reasons, and one imam expressed his personal preference to avoid conducting polygamous marriages.

> We avoid conducting polygamous marriages, primarily because it conflicts with English law, and because it can be unjust in the way it is practised among British Muslims, contrary to the way encouraged in the Quran, so they abuse it, and the wives are left without legal redress.
>
> (SC Judge #1)

> To date I have not conducted a polygamous marriage, but if asked I would avoid performing the *nikah*, as many people who practice polygamy do so without justice.
>
> (Imam #1)

Overall the participants did not have any aversion to civil marriage, many participants had transnational marriages and needed a legally valid marriage to make immigration applications for their spouses. Participants with *nikah*-only marriage explained their reasons: for some, it was a personal choice, others expected a civil registration after the *nikah* but it never occurred, whilst some did not see the need to register as their spouses were already British nationals.

> I just had an Islamic marriage. Not bothered with a civil [registry], because it's my second marriage. It's irrelevant.
>
> (Rushna)

> I wanted a registry. He [the husband] kept saying it's not necessary, but I know that in this country it is necessary. He didn't want to do it.
>
> (Jahanara)

> He [new husband] was born and brought up in the UK. He was a divorcee and has a child from the previous marriage. He loves my children like his own.
>
> (Parvin)

The professionals expressed concerns regarding unregistered marriages among their clients, especially the lack of legal protections, rights and access to family courts during a marital breakdown.

> Non-registration is a problem. They have no legal rights.
>
> (Imam #2)

> In *nikah*-only marriages, the women are cohabitees or girlfriends. They have to prove their contribution to the marriage [if they break up]. They are throwing away their opportunity to justice.
>
> (Solicitor #2)

Also, the Shariah Council raised concerns regarding unregistered marriage, as observed during a *nikah* ceremony conducted on their premises.

> The judge asked the couple if they are going to civil register the marriage. The man looked bewildered and glanced towards his new bride … The man then said to the judge 'probably not'. The judge said 'why not?' He reminded them that they could not access the civil courts in the future if they have marital disputes. The couple did not discuss this any further and left the room happily married.
>
> (PO7)

Whilst civil marriage may not constitute an Islamic marriage among British Muslims, to have a civil registered marriage and subsequently any civil divorce could be relevant when pursuing an Islamic divorce as discussed in the next section.

Divorce

There are three main forms of Islamic divorce: *talaq*, *khula* and *faskh*. *Talaq* refers to a husband's right to unilateral divorce, whereas *khula* is a means for the wife to be released from the marriage, and *faskh* is dissolution at the bequest of a Shariah authority, such as an Islamic scholar or Shariah Council.[26] A key difference between *talaq* and *khula* is that in the case of *talaq* the husband must ensure full payment of the dower and thus financially more advantageous for women, whereas with *khula* as the wife requested the divorce, she may, in turn, have to return the dower to the husband. Both these forms of divorces according to classical interpretations of Islamic law can be extra-judicial, though Muslim-majority countries regulate Islamic divorce as part of their personal status law.[27] Moreover, extra-judicial divorce (e.g. *talaq*) has been invalid in Britain since the passing of the Domicile and Matrimonial Proceedings Act 1973, and matters relating to divorce and children are exclusively legislated by civil law.[28]

Nonetheless, civil law does not resolve religious divorce, thus, the guidelines for petitioning a civil divorce highlight that divorce proceedings may not dissolve the religious part of the marriage.[29] This, in turn, creates a further problem for British Muslims, especially where the husband may withhold the religious divorce, as was the case with many participants who attained a civil divorce certificate and pursued an Islamic divorce. Participants explained the importance of Islamic divorce to them.

> To hear *talaq* meant it was official, you've severed the link with them [in-laws].
>
> (Faiza)

> Otherwise, people think you are still married.
>
> (Fahima)

> Religious divorce is more important to me. I needed freedom I needed my sanity.
>
> (Henna)

Research shows that Muslims turn to religious frameworks and norms, for personal needs, and during a crisis, e.g. divorce.[30] Muslims may seek a religious divorce even after a civil divorce as the Muslim community may not recognise secular divorce.[31] The problem of men withholding religious divorce can also be found in the Jewish faith whereby orthodox Jewish women refused the 'get' (Jewish divorce) are labelled 'agunah' or 'anchored woman', similar to how Muslim women after a civil divorce can be in a 'limping marriage'.[32] Under the Divorce (Religious Marriages) Act 2002, the judge can refuse to issue the decree absolutely until the religious divorce is resolved; however, this act is currently only applicable to the Jewish faith, though others have called for the Muslim faith to also be prescribed.[33] Yet others believe Shariah Councils have effectively resolved the problem of withholding religious divorce by granting *faskh*.[34] One participant with an unregistered marriage explained her situation.

During mediation, I asked my husband to give me divorce [*talaq*]. He said he will not give me a divorce. I asked him 'why not?' He wouldn't answer me. I told him, it is more difficult for women to apply for divorce, whereas you can say it in front of witnesses and it is done. He said 'I'm not going to do it.' Later, I found out why it is because he did not want to give me back my gold [*mahr*].

(Jahanara)

Bano views imams as a linkage between mosques and Shariah Councils, who also act as mediators resolving marital disputes.[35] The experts mentioned the use of imams, counsellors or Shariah Councils was usually the last resort, and even then the clients may not reconcile.

People come to the imam or the mosque after they have tried to rectify the situation on their own. They would incorporate their family and trusted friends. The last resort would be to involve the imam.

(Imam #1)

The majority of clients [that come to the Sharia Council] do not reconcile. It is nice when it happens, but it is rare.

(SC Judge #1)

Mediation was not common among the participants, who described that their husbands refused mediation or the families including the in-laws objected to the involvement of an outsider. Shah-Kazemi contends mediation is rarely pursued, husbands often refuse mediation denying any problems in the marriage.[36] Even so, two participants mentioned the use of imams in resolving their disputes. One participant found the imam was unable to persuade the husband to agree to *khula*, who was stalling the divorce process. In another case, the imam told the participant that she did not have sufficient grounds to seek *khula*.

We got the imam from the local mosque involved. The imam tried to mediate between us. My husband said he had no money and that he was feeling stressed. It was a case where he was not going to give the divorce.

(Rahima)

My family called the imam from the mosque. He came and listened to my case, but said that I was at fault, I was shocked, and that my husband was a good man. The mosque did not agree to give me an Islamic divorce.

(Lubna)

These two cases demonstrate the extent of an imam's authority, firstly a limitation, by not granting *khula* without the husband's consent, and secondly, overriding powers to deny *khula* in dismissing the wife's request. However, each case of *khula* may present a different outcome depending on the circumstances, though one imam commented where the husband refuses to grant a religious divorce, there is a need for a greater authority.

[Islamic] divorce has two aspects: mediation and the execution of divorce – the latter is a collective duty and requires a Sharia board. When the husband refuses to divorce a woman, where do they go? This is when they turn to a Sharia Council.

(Imam #2)

In alleviating the situation of withheld religious divorce, one of the imams viewed that the civil divorce was sufficient as an Islamic divorce, and no further action was required from either party. He cited the Hanafi School as evidence.

If they've obtained the civil divorce, even if the wife was the petitioner, and the husband signs the papers then it is consent; and in the Hanafi opinion Islamically they are divorced already. So they don't really need to go through the Islamic divorce process but people still want to do that because they want to get a sense of comfort that they've gone through the Islamic way. So they can get some advice and guidance on what they can do after a civil divorce.

(Imam #1)

Others argue that civil divorce is not valid as an Islamic divorce, and go to the extent of issuing a *fatwa* (religious edict) that non-Muslims have no jurisdiction in the matter,[37] thus adding confusion for those who have already obtained a civil divorce.

Shariah Councils

Shariah Councils are quasi-legal or unofficial legal bodies that function to mediate, arbitrate and issue Muslim divorce certificates: the product of transnational networks unique to the British diaspora.[38] Other studies in Western countries such as France, Canada, the United States of America and Australia confirm that Muslims there also refer marital disputes to Shariah Councils,[39] albeit these institutions are not as structured as the Shariah Councils found in Britain. Shariah Councils emerged out of public interest (*maslahah*) within the British Muslim community to fill the vacuum in resolving women's religious divorce.[40] The Shariah Council explained that their clients were mainly women.

> Ninety per cent of our cases are women-initiated divorce. Women come to us because they want verification that they are divorced because their husband pronounced divorce (*talaq*), or they started the civil proceedings and want the Islamic divorce. In other cases, women have no civil marriage and come to us [Sharia Council] as they have nowhere else to go to get a divorce.
>
> (SC Judge #1)

There are reports that at least 85 Shariah Councils are operating as parallel legal systems, though mainly out of mosques around the country.[41] Bano reports a more conservative figure of 30 Shariah Councils and concludes that these councils do not desire to replace civil law, and claims of forming a parallel legal system are unfounded.[42] The imams commented on the perception of Shariah Councils and their role in society.

> When you hear of Sharia courts [i.e. councils], the perception is there are many operating out there, yet there are only a few main ones across the country. The rest are one or two people in the mosque dealing with cases, I do not think they are genuine courts.
>
> (Imam #2)

> All the Sharia Councils operate in an advisory capacity, they have no legal remit, and they can't enforce anything. They only provide pastoral care, Islamic guidance, more theory than anything else, in my opinion, and that is enough.
>
> (Imam #1)

The imams reiterated two issues: firstly, that in reality there are probably a small number of organisations genuinely set up to act as Shariah Councils operating in Britain, and secondly, the modus operandi of these councils is only in an advisory capacity. Furthermore, the Shariah Council's documentation – application forms and information sheets – clearly demarcates their limitations with respect to civil law, for instance, they state that all civil marriages including overseas marriages require a civil divorce for dissolution, and refer clients to solicitors for civil divorce cases. The Shariah Council explained that they do not adjudicate on matters concerning child arrangements and financial relief.

> We deal with religious divorce and *mahr* only. Anything else the parties have to go to family courts or small claim courts for settlement, we cannot deal with this.
>
> (SC Judge #1)

Another concern raised against Shariah Councils is the oppression of women with religiously sanctioned gender discrimination[43] and the application of Shariah law which contradicts universal human rights.[44] Norton argues that religious tribunals support religious freedom, as they are a source of religious knowledge and guidance; and religious expertise is an important aspect of religious freedom.[45] The Islamic divorce process with the Shariah Council differentiated between male- and female-initiated divorce. In *talaq* applications, the council's role was one of administering the process. Whereas the *khula* application was more arduous, applicants had to justify their reasons for divorce, the process could take longer to complete and involved more fees than the *talaq*. One participant with a *nikah*-only marriage explained her frustration with the Shariah Council.

> He [the husband] said he was never going to give me a divorce. So I asked my cousin, he's a *Hafiz* [memorised Quran], he said, 'apply to the Sharia Council they will help you.' So, I applied to the Sharia Council; I thought the fee was too much, and they said the process could take 6–9 months, I was agitated by this because they delayed my certificate. But they understood me and agreed to dissolve the marriage, which they did.
>
> (Jahanara)

The necessity for an authoritative Shariah body to proclaim *faskh* leads British Muslims to approach mosques and Shariah Councils who have a panel or Shariah board to consider their divorce cases. Qureshi's study of marital breakdown among British Asians found the bulk of the cases dealt with by Shariah Councils were *faskhs*, i.e. dissolutions, and believes it is a sign of the unwillingness of men to recognise the authority of Shariah Council.[46] However, in this study, the Shariah Council often declared *faskh* due to the unwillingness of men to release women from the marriage, not because the husbands rejected the Council's authority, a subtle difference. The Shariah Council provided further explanation.

> To men it is an affront if a woman remarries; it is like how dare she moves on. Men are withholding *talaq* when they have every right to give the wife *talaq*. The man gets annoyed that someone else can give a divorce certificate so that he cannot be spiteful anymore.
>
> (SC Judge #1)

For this function alone, *faskh*, Shariah Councils provide an important role among the British diasporic Muslim community which the civil authorities are unable to provide, i.e. religious divorce. In general, the experts viewed Shariah Councils contributed positively to securing Islamic divorce for Muslim women; though they accepted not all Shariah Councils processed divorce efficiently and there was scope to improve their procedures and infrastructure.

> There is nothing wrong with the motive of the existing services [Sharia Councils], but maybe they lack the appropriate measures and appropriate application, it is quite challenging.
>
> (Imam #2)

The Shariah Council explained how they worked in cohesion with other services such as the police, solicitors and counsellors; though their services face constant scrutiny by the media and government, the Shariah Council argued there is a need for the specialist services they provide to the Muslim community. The experts agreed Shariah Councils could improve practices by addressing gender-related issues such as the disparity in application fees for *talaq* and *khula* and having female caseworkers and female members on the Shariah board. The Shariah Council responded on the issue of fees.

> [Sharia Council] judges give decisions according to the situation. No woman is refused a divorce, rather it takes time to process an application. And where there are financial difficulties, women receiving [welfare] benefits are entitled to concessions on the fees.
>
> (SC Judge #3)

Whilst Shariah Councils are imperfect in their current form with room for improvement, they fill a void in civil law by resolving religious divorce. The findings of this study suggest the need to establish a 'standard of practice' to ensure equality and justice among forums that resolve Islamic divorce. Firstly, Shariah Councils that recognise a civil divorce as sufficient and issue an Islamic divorce accordingly represent the best option for women seeking religious divorce. Secondly, there needs to be equality in the application process for Islamic divorce, whereby fees charged to men and women are the same, and the length of time to process the application is consistent. Thirdly, Shariah Councils need to incorporate a complaints procedure and appeals system concerning decisions given to ensure justice and transparency. Fourthly, female representation is required at different levels of the application process, from female caseworkers to female members on the Shariah board or decision-making panel. Adopting these recommendations would ensure Shariah Councils and other similar forums safeguard and empower women and address any imbalances arising from norms that disadvantage Muslim women.

Conclusion

This chapter examined the lived realities of marriage and divorce among British Muslims and highlighted the importance of *nikah* in establishing the marriage and Islamic divorce to end a marriage. The insights gained from the professionals and the observation of the Shariah Council show they have an awareness of the civil law and provide services accordingly. Civil marriage was recommended to provide Muslim women protection and rights, and access to civil courts in the event of a marital breakdown. Also, a civil divorce could be relevant where a Shariah Council accepts it as evidencing a religious divorce. However, for many women and religious establishments, the Islamic divorce supersedes any civil divorce, and therefore the reforms and regulations proposed in this chapter seek to improve standards among Shariah Councils and other forums that provide services to Muslim women seeking an Islamic divorce.

Notes

1 Samia Bano, *Muslim Women and Shari'ah Councils: Transcending the Boundaries of Community and Law* (Palgrave Macmillan 2012) 84.
2 Pragna Patel, 'Sharia Courts Have No Place in UK Family Law. Listen to Women Who Know' *The Guardian* (London, 14 December 2016); Elham

Manea, *Women and Sharia Law: The Impact of Legal Pluralism in the UK* (I.B. Tauris 2016).

3 Gillian Douglas, Norman Doe, Sophie Gilliat-Ray, Russell Sandberg, and Asma Khan, *Social Cohesion and Religious Law: Marriage, Divorce and Religious Courts* (Cardiff Law School 2011).

4 Sara Khan, 'Muslim Marriages Like George Galloway's Should Be Registered' *The Guardian* (London, 4 May 2012).

5 Home Office, 'The Independent Review into the Application of Sharia Law in England and Wales' (2018) <https://www.gov.uk/government/publications/applying-sharia-law-in-england-and-wales-independent-review> accessed 2 September 2020.

6 Farrah Ahmed and Jane Calderwood Norton, 'Religious Tribunals, Religious Freedom, and Concern for Vulnerable Women' 24 *Child and Family Law Quarterly* 363, 2012.

7 Patel; Manea Maryam Namazie, Yassi Atasheen, Anna Waters, and Muriel Seltman, *Sharia Law in Britain: A Threat to One Law for All & Equal Rights* (One Law for All 2010).

8 Maleiha Malik, *Minority Legal Orders in the UK: Minorities, Pluralism and the Law* (The British Academy 2012).

9 Home Office, 'Independent Review into Sharia Law Launched' (2016) <https://www.gov.uk/government/news/independent-review-into-sharia-law-launched> accessed 2 September 2020.

10 Home Office, 'The Independent Review into the Application of Sharia Law in England and Wales'.

11 Home Office, 'Faith Practices: Written statement - HCWS442' (2018) <https://www.parliament.uk/business/publications/written-questions-answers-statements/written-statement/Commons/2018-02-01/HCWS442/> accessed 2 September 2020.

12 ONS, *2011 Census* (Office for National Statistics 2011).

13 Sophie Gilliat-Ray, *Muslims in Britain* (Cambridge University Press 2010).

14 Edward E Curtis, IV (ed) *Encyclopedia of Muslim-American History* (Infobase Publishing 2010) 154.

15 Tariq Ramadan, *Western Muslims and the Future of Islam* (Oxford University Press 2004) 139.

16 Rebecca Probert, 'The Evolving Concept of Non-Marriage' 25 *Child and Family Law Quarterly* 314, 2013.

17 Ramadan 139–140; Habiba Jaan, *Equal and Free? 50 Muslim Women's Experiences of Marriage in Britain Today* (Aurat 2014).

18 Ahmed and Norton.

19 Arbitration and Mediation Services (Equality) Bill (2016–17) Marriage Act 1949 (Amendment) Bill (2017–19).

20 Home Office, 'The Independent Review into the Application of Sharia Law in England and Wales'.

21 Rakesh Kumar Singh, *Textbook on Muslim Law* (Universal Law Publishing 2011).

22 Judith E Tucker, *Women, Family, and Gender in Islamic Law* (Cambridge University Press 2008).

23 Ann Laquer Estin, 'Unofficial Family Law' 94 *Iowa Law Review* 449, 2008; Anika Liversage, 'Secrets and Lies: When Ethnic Minority Have

Nikah' in Prakash Shah, Marie-Claire Foblets and Mathias Rohe (eds), *Family, Religion and Law: Cultural Encounters in Europe* (Ashgate Publishing Ltd 2014).

24 Ann Black, 'In the Shadow of Our Legal System: Shari'a in Australia' in Rex J Ahdar and Nicholas Aroney (eds), *Shari'a in the West* (Oxford University Press 2010); Julie Macfarlane, *Islamic Divorce in North America: A Shari'a Path in a Secular Society* (Oxford University Press 2012).

25 Rajnaara C Akhtar, 'Unregistered Muslim Marriages: An Emerging Culture of Celebrating Rites and Compromising Rights' in JK Miles, P Mody and R Probert (eds), *Marriage Rites and Rights* (Bloomsbury Publishing 2015).

26 John L Esposito and Natana J DeLong-Bas, *Women in Muslim Family Law* (2nd edn, Syracuse University Press 2001); Raffia Arshad, *Islamic Family Law* (Sweet & Maxwell/Thomson Reuters 2010).

27 Abdullahi Ahmed An-Naim (ed), *Islamic Family Law in a Changing World: A Global Resource Book* (Zed Books 2002).

28 Elizabeth Butler-Sloss and Mark Hill, 'Family Law: Current Conflicts and Their Resolution' in Robin Griffith-Jones (ed), *Islam and English Law: Rights, Responsibilities, and the Place of Shari'a* (Cambridge University Press 2013).

29 Crown, *D008 Supporting Notes for Guidance on Completing a Divorce/Dissolution/(Judicial) Separation Petition* (HM Courts & Tribunals Service 2014).

30 Curtis Macfarlane.

31 Ihsan Yilmaz, 'The Challenge of Post-Modern Legality and Muslim Legal Pluralism in England' 28 *Journal of Ethnic and Migration Studies* 343, 2002; Jemma Wilson, 'Sharia Debate in Britain: Sharia Councils and the Oppression of Muslim Women' 1 *The Aberdeen Student Law Review* 46, 2010.

32 Nigel V Lowe and Gillian Douglas, *Bromley's Family Law* (Oxford University Press 2015); David Pearl and Werner Menski, *Muslim Family Law* (3rd edn, Sweet & Maxwell 1998).

33 Charlotte Proudman, 'Religious Marriages: Staying a Decree Absolute in Order to Increase the Chances of Obtaining a Religious Divorce' (*Family Law Week*, 2013) <http://www.familylawweek.co.uk/site.aspx?i=ed111039> accessed 2 September 2020; Ahmed and Norton Shaista Gohir, 'Listening to Muslim Women on Sharia Divorce Could Change It for the Better' *The Guardian* (London, 1 November 2016).

34 Federica Sona, 'Defending the Family Treasure Chest: Navigating Muslim Families and Secured Positivistic Islands of European Legal Systems' in Prakash Shah, Marie-Claire Foblets and Mathias Rohe (eds), *Family, Religion and Law: Cultural Encounters in Europe* (Ashgate Publishing Ltd 2014).

35 Bano 92.

36 SN Shah-Kazemi, *Untying the Knot: Muslim Women, Divorce and the Shariah* (The Nuffield Foundation 2001) 56.

37 Haitham Al-Haddad, 'Fatwa: A Civil Divorce Is Not a Valid Islamic Divorce' (2010) <https://www.islam21c.com/fataawa/912-fatwa-a-civil-divorce-is-not-a-valid-islamic-divorce/> accessed 2 September 2020; Muhammad Saalih Al-Munajjid, 'Documenting Divorce in a Civil, Non-Islamic Court' (*Islam QA*, 2010) <https://islamqa.info/en/answers/

142953/documenting-divorce-in-a-civil-non-islamic-court> accessed 2 September 2020.

38 Bano 84.
39 Macfarlane Ghena Krayem, *Islamic Family Law in Australia ISS 16: To Recognise or Not to Recognise* (Melbourne University Publishing 2014).
40 John R Bowen, *On British Islam: Religion, Law, and Everyday Practice in Shari'a Councils* (Princeton University Press 2016) 47.
41 Denis MacEoin, *Sharia Law Or 'One Law for All?'* (Civitas 2009) 69.
42 S Bano, *An Exploratory Study of Shariah Councils in England with Respect to Family Law* (Ministry of Justice and the University of Reading 2012) 15.
43 Caroline Cox, *A Parallel World: Confronting the Abuse of Many Muslim Women in Britain Today* (The Bow Group 2015).
44 Manea.
45 JC Norton, *The Freedom of Religious Organizations* (Oxford University Press 2016) 43.
46 K Qureshi, *Marital Breakdown among British Asians: Conjugality, Legal Pluralism and New Kinship* (Palgrave Macmillan 2016) 172.

Bibliography

Arbitration and Mediation Services (Equality) Bill (2016–17).
Ahmed F and Norton JC, 'Religious Tribunals, Religious Freedom, and Concern for Vulnerable Women' 24 *Child and Family Law Quarterly* 363, 2012.
Akhtar RC, 'Unregistered Muslim Marriages: An Emerging Culture of Celebrating Rites and Compromising Rights' in Miles JK, Mody P and Probert R (eds), *Marriage Rites and Rights* (Bloomsbury Publishing 2015).
Al-Haddad H, 'Fatwa: A Civil Divorce Is Not a Valid Islamic Divorce' (2010) <https://www.islam21c.com/fataawa/912-fatwa-a-civil-divorce-is-not-a-valid-islamic-divorce/> accessed 2 September 2020.
Al-Munajjid MS, 'Documenting Divorce in a Civil, Non-Islamic Court' (*Islam QA*, 2010) <https://islamqa.info/en/answers/142953/documenting-divorce-in-a-civil-non-islamic-court> accessed 2 September 2020.
An-Naim AA (ed) *Islamic Family Law in a Changing World: A Global Resource Book* (Zed Books 2002).
Arshad R, *Islamic Family Law* (Sweet & Maxwell/Thomson Reuters 2010).
Bano S, *An Exploratory Study of Shariah Councils in England with Respect to Family Law* (Ministry of Justice and the University of Reading 2012).
——, *Muslim Women and Shari'ah Councils: Transcending the Boundaries of Community and Law* (Palgrave Macmillan 2012).
Black A, 'In the Shadow of Our Legal System: Shari'a in Australia' in Ahdar RJ and Aroney N (eds), *Shari'a in the West* (Oxford University Press 2010).
Bowen JR, *On British Islam: Religion, Law, and Everyday Practice in Shari'a Councils* (Princeton University Press 2016).
Butler-Sloss E and Hill M, 'Family Law: Current Conflicts and Their Resolution' in Griffith-Jones R (ed), *Islam and English Law: Rights, Responsibilities, and the Place of Shari'a* (Cambridge University Press 2013).

Cox C, *A Parallel World: Confronting the Abuse of Many Muslim Women in Britain Today* (The Bow Group 2015).

Crown, *D008 Supporting Notes for Guidance on Completing a Divorce/Dissolution/(Judicial) Separation Petition* (HM Courts & Tribunals Service 2014).

Curtis EE, IV (ed) *Encyclopedia of Muslim-American History* (Infobase Publishing 2010).

Divorce (Religious Marriages) Act.

Domicile and Matrimonial Proceedings Act.

Douglas G Doe, N, Gilliat-Ray, S, Sandberg, R, Khan, A, *Social Cohesion and Religious Law: Marriage, Divorce and Religious Courts* (Cardiff Law School 2011).

Equality Act.

Esposito JL and DeLong-Bas NJ, *Women in Muslim Family Law* (2nd edn, Syracuse University Press 2001).

Estin AL, 'Unofficial Family Law' 94 *Iowa Law Review* 449, 2008.

Gilliat-Ray S, *Muslims in Britain* (Cambridge University Press 2010).

Gohir S, 'Listening to Muslim Women on Sharia Divorce Could Change It for the Better' *The Guardian* (London, 1 November 2016).

Home Office, 'Independent Review into Sharia Law Launched' (2016) <https://www.gov.uk/government/news/independent-review-into-sharia-law-launched> accessed 2 September 2020.

———, 'Faith Practices: Written statement - HCWS442' (2018) <https://www.parliament.uk/business/publications/written-questions-answers-statements/written-statement/Commons/2018-02-01/HCWS442/> accessed 2 September 2020.

———, 'The Independent Review into the Application of Sharia Law in England and Wales' (2018) <https://www.gov.uk/government/publications/applying-sharia-law-in-england-and-wales-independent-review> accessed 2 September 2020.

Jaan H, *Equal and Free? 50 Muslim Women's Experiences of Marriage in Britain Today* (Aurat 2014).

Khan S, 'Muslim Marriages Like George Galloway's Should Be Registered' *The Guardian* (London, 4 May 2012).

Krayem G, *Islamic Family Law in Australia ISS 16: To Recognise Or Not to Recognise* (Melbourne University Publishing 2014).

Liversage A, 'Secrets and Lies: When Ethnic Minority Have Nikah' in Shah P, Foblets M-C and Rohe M (eds), *Family, Religion and Law: Cultural Encounters in Europe* (Ashgate Publishing Ltd 2014).

Lowe NV and Douglas G, *Bromley's Family Law* (Oxford University Press 2015).

MacEoin D, *Sharia Law Or 'One Law for All?'* (Civitas 2009).

Macfarlane J, *Islamic Divorce in North America: A Shari'a Path in a Secular Society* (Oxford University Press 2012).

Malik M, *Minority Legal Orders in the UK: Minorities, Pluralism and the Law* (The British Academy 2012).

Manea E, *Women and Sharia Law: The Impact of Legal Pluralism in the UK* (I.B. Tauris 2016).

Marriage Act.

Marriage Act 1949 (Amendment) Bill (2017–19).

Matrimonial Causes Act.

Namazie M, Atasheen, Y, Waters, A, and Seltman, M, *Sharia Law in Britain: A Threat to One Law for All & Equal Rights* (One Law for All 2010).

Norton JC, *The Freedom of Religious Organizations* (Oxford University Press 2016).

ONS, *2011 Census* (Office for National Statistics 2011).

Patel P, 'Sharia Courts Have No Place in UK Family Law. Listen to Women Who Know' *The Guardian* (London, 14 December 2016).

Pearl D and Menski W, *Muslim Family Law* (3rd edn, Sweet & Maxwell 1998).

Probert R, 'The Evolving Concept of Non-Marriage' 25 *Child and Family Law Quarterly* 314, 2013.

Proudman C, 'Religious Marriages: Staying a Decree Absolute in Order to Increase the Chances of Obtaining a Religious Divorce' (*Family Law Week*, 2013) <http://www.familylawweek.co.uk/site.aspx?i=ed111039> accessed 2 September 2020.

Qureshi K, *Marital Breakdown among British Asians: Conjugality, Legal Pluralism and New Kinship* (Palgrave Macmillan 2016).

Ramadan T, *Western Muslims and the Future of Islam* (Oxford University Press 2004).

Shah-Kazemi SN, *Untying the Knot: Muslim Women, Divorce and the Shariah* (The Nuffield Foundation 2001).

Singh RK, *Textbook on Muslim Law* (Universal Law Publishing 2011).

Sona F, 'Defending the Family Treasure Chest: Navigating Muslim Families and Secured Positivistic Islands of European Legal Systems' in Shah P, Foblets M-C and Rohe M (eds), *Family, Religion and Law: Cultural Encounters in Europe* (Ashgate Publishing Ltd 2014).

Tucker JE, *Women, Family, and Gender in Islamic Law* (Cambridge University Press 2008).

Wilson J, 'Sharia Debate in Britain: Sharia Councils and the Oppression of Muslim Women' 1 *The Aberdeen Student Law Review* 46, 2010.

Yilmaz I, 'The Challenge of Post-Modern Legality and Muslim Legal Pluralism in England' 28 *Journal of Ethnic and Migration Studies* 343, 2002.

4 Domestic Abuse

The Dichotomy of Choosing between Informal and Formal Forum for Mediation, Arbitration and Justice

Naheed Ghauri

Introduction

In domestic abuse, a woman's freedom is inhibited and negative freedom sets in 'negative freedom is when a woman is abused and barred from leaving her home based on a negative freedom model (Hirschmann, 2013:58) or develops a 'battered woman's syndrome'', and such a situation complicates freedom (Walker, 2017). In this chapter, we find that Muslim women are not essentialised or their experiences are generalised into a single mould, as Muslim women who align themselves with Islam inhabit various sectarian, ideological and analytical understanding of Islam. Rather, the author uses this to qualify the identity of women who not only subscribe to the faith but actively see themselves as 'practising' it (in whichever form they do so).

The family courts under the Practice Direction 12J (Family Procedure Rules, PD12J – Child Arrangements and Contact: Domestic Abuse and Harm, Family Procedure Rules (8 December 2017)) adopted a revised definition to include dowry-related abuse, honour-based abuse and transnational marriage abandonment.[1] However, the Domestic Abuse Act 2021 introduces a new statutory definition to be gender-neutral and compliant to the Istanbul Convention.

Domestic abuse cases present the most intractable forms of power imbalances between couples when conducting mediation. The scope of this chapter is limited to discussion in the context of heterosexual domestic relationships focusing on Muslim women.[2] The existence of violence-based and other imbalances of power in homosexual relationships is acknowledged. This chapter proceeds on the assumption that the issue of domestic abuse itself cannot be mediated. Domestic

DOI: 10.4324/9781003090410-5

abuse issues highlight the need to consider ways in which mediators can begin to mitigate this navigation of power and respond to cultural difference in ethical ways (Brigg, 2008:52). Morgan Brigg (2008) argues that in Western mediation practice, conflict and violence are typically seen as destructive and unhelpful, and this attitude precludes the constitutive and productive role that mediation plays in many non-Western traditions and particularly the emergence of Islamic mediation in North America and England (Brigg, 2008:287; Abdalla, 2001). Brigg (2008:292) draws upon Michel Foucault's (1982) conception of 'power' to the application in mediation.[3] Foucault's (1982) hypothesis of 'power struggle' asserts that it is impossible to separate power from social relations, for example, in family relations. English family law can to some extent address gender inequalities and power imbalances, but law is not entirely gender conscious (Webley, 2017). Therefore power imbalances cannot be completely ruled out in family relations with unequal powers and it is bound to happen between parties (not always in favour of men) in an informal non-state setting, for example, disputes being resolved using faith-based dispute resolution such as Shari'a Councils.

British Muslim women are better informed about gender equality, but some choose to live by patriarchal customs (Okin, 1999). Susan Moller Okin (1999) argues that most cultural and religious groups, including minorities within the West, often limit and harm women, particularly where they are concerned with keeping male power over women. For example, setting conditions such as restricting the amount of financial entitlement (such as *mahr*, or property share which is common for British Muslims) in Islamic marriage contract often creates an additional power imbalance between husband and wife, and Okin (1999) argues that to grant patriarchal cultural groups special rights would ignore the wellbeing of women. In private family relations, if inequality and patriarchy is part and parcel of the household and abuse against women, then media, religion and education is not likely to promote equality between parties (Bano, 2012; Webley, 2017).

Muslim women continue to choose religious arbitration and mediation because they need a religious divorce (there are different types of divorces depending upon who instigates it and on the circumstances), recovery of *mahr* (nuptial gift) and/or Islamic arbitration. Therefore, this chapter proposes reforms for Muslim women in the following key areas: domestic abuse, litigants in person/lack of funding, religious authority and enhancement of mediation models based on egalitarian principles and/or an integrated co-mediator model (consisting of English and Islamic mediator). Setting up safeguards under Islamic mediation and referring both vulnerable men and women to a panel of co-mediators (English and Islamic) for better screening will also lead to better compliance with mediation principles under English family law, particularly the Family Mediation Council's (FMC) Code of Practice because this does not conflict with Islamic principles.[4]

The Home Office Report (2018)[5] shed some light on the provision of advice in Islamic family disputes and the common issues of concern were gender inequalities, lax approaches to domestic abuse and violence, absence of child safeguarding mechanisms and ignoring mediation principles under English family law, the FMC's Code of Practice. However, the 2018 report did not specifically deal with the causes of power imbalances in depth, particularly the underlying causes. Instead it examined discrimination suffered and how this can be eliminated within Shari'a Councils. Discrimination and injustices generate considerable amounts of publicity and criticism when exposed and it brings into question whether the informal system is compatible with English legal principles (Griffith-Jones, 2013).[6] This approach ignores the underlying problem that Islamic family law is not homogenous or codified and studies such as those of Elham Manea confirm that it adopts non-egalitarian principles (Manea, 2016). Ziba Mir-Hosseini (2015) proposes a constructive solution by adopting egalitarian Muslim family law which places gender justice at the core of Islamic legal tradition. This can assist to overcome not only the external criticisms but also internal problems of power and gender imbalances when taking account of gender and justice (Bano, 2012). This means that there can be integration of specific elements of egalitarian principles of Islamic mediation into the general framework of mediation with certain safeguards in place to deliver a fair outcome, for example, in a co-mediation model (Islamic and English mediator). Islamic mediation without safeguards conflicts with English legal principles of mediation (voluntary, confidential, impartial and suitable) and this can be found in the FMC's Code of Conduct[7] and safeguards for victims of domestic abuse which exempts mediation (Family Procedure Rules 2010, (FPR) 3.8 (1)/(2)). While these safeguards can provide security to victims of abuse, it does not eliminate power imbalances completely.

Pre-mediation Assessment and English Mediation

There is a general requirement for couples to attend MIAM (Mediation Assessment Information Meeting), a pre-mediation assessment before issuing an application for a financial order or child-related orders (section 10 (3) of the Children and Families Act 2014). MIAMs are important safeguards in domestic abuse cases and if this procedure is followed by Shari'a Councils then it would certainly assist to protect vulnerable victims of abuse at risk under MIAM exemptions (FPR 3.8 (1)/(2)) and recent scholarship examines power imbalances in mediation and how different models can minimise this (Maclean and Eekelaar, 2016; Webley, 2017). There can be problems if adequate assessment of the circumstances is not conducted at the initial MIAM and the matter proceeds to mediation which could result in power imbalances.

If, after attending MIAM, the parties wish to proceed with mediation and their suitability has been assessed then mediation takes place. The English law mediation process is a formal forum governed by four principles set out in the FMC Code of Practice: mediation is voluntary (FMC Code of Practice, 5.2) and both parties and the mediator must agree mediation is suitable (FMC Code of Practice, 5.3); the mediator is impartial and facilitates negotiation and has no vested interest in the outcome (FMC of Code of Practice, 5.4); mediation is confidential except where there are concerns of risk of harm to a child or vulnerable adult (FMC Code of Practice, 5.5); and the decision-making rests with the parties. These principles are important because Shari'a Councils are not always observing these principles such as impartiality and concerns of risk of harm, especially where scholars are disregarding domestic abuse issues and pursue mediation and reconciliation without considering further harm it may cause women and children. Several scholars have addressed domestic abuse and power imbalances in private forum and how to manage mediation in these circumstances using different types of mediation approaches, but it is beyond the scope of this chapter to explore this (Hester and Pearson, 1997; Maclean and Eekelaar, 2016; Webley, 2017).

Methodology

This chapter uses qualitative research (grounded theory (Glaser and Strauss, 1967:1)) and focus groups (Calder, 1977). Data is drawn principally from semi-structured in-depth face-to-face interviews with 30 Muslim women. Of the 30 women, 25 were individually interviewed and five women from a focus group (aged between 18 and 55) between 2012 and 2016. These were women who were victims of abuse and attended Islamic arbitration, mediation sessions at the Shari'a Councils or mediation with English mediators. Women interviewed were sub-divided into four demographic categories: educational background; registered/unregistered/polygamous marriages (these were in registered and polygamous marriages); British/non-British (these were settled national immigrants with valid leave to remain such as spouse, student or visitor visa and immigrants without valid leave to remain such as over-stayers or failed asylum seekers); and the Islamic school followed (all practising Muslims). The languages spoken were: English, Arabic, Farsi, Pashtu, Pothwari, Urdu, Bengali and Punjabi; and interpreters were only required for Arabic, Pothwari and Farsi/Pashtu. The interviews were conducted in the following cities: London, Bolton, Manchester, Southampton, Portsmouth, Bournemouth, Leicester and Wolverhampton. These women agreed to share their experiences of Shari'a Councils, English mediators and civil family courts. Interviews focused on mediation experiences at Shari'a Councils and with English mediators, and questioned encounters of discrimination, power imbalances, desirable outcomes achieved, conduct of the mediators, understanding of their problem and procedural information given. Pseudonyms were used for the interviewees. Thematic analysis of data was undertaken.

The empirical research conducted was intended to ascertain how views relating to mediation are reached by Muslim women on whether or not to enter mediation, their basis and beliefs, and, particularly, power imbalance sources. Participants were selected using practitioner-based cases (these were through direct contact with participants in practice undergoing mediation sessions with Shari'a Councils and English mediators and indirect contact with participants who had already gone through mediation sessions) and snowballing technique to recruit participants (Hesse-Biber and Leavy, 2006). Snowballing technique is when existing women would refer others as potential participants. Snowball effect helped to generate further participants and to maximise potential recruits to the research. The fieldwork involved handling very sensitive data, all the ethical standards professionally and from an academic research perspective, including confidentiality.[8]

The aim was to interview as many individuals from as many diverse backgrounds as possible to present original and new findings. Following established protocols on conducting ethical research (requiring informed consent, translations provided in Arabic/Farsi to participants and respecting confidentiality), interviews were recorded and lasted one-two hours each. When interpreting interview transcripts, each narrative was examined based on close readings of statements. Statements made by participants were grouped into themes using discourse analysis (which is a study of written and spoken language in relation to its social context), representing emerging themes, ideas and the content that the researcher thought was particularly significant (Gee and Handford, 2013). There were searches conducted on any connections between topics discussed, what was significant to each participant, what was frequently said and there was analysis of how one theme in one interview transcript related to another transcript. The emerging themes were then organised and further explored in order to provide a coherent overview of the findings from the data.

There are limitations to this method. In this chapter's research, victims of abuse (these were victims who suffered physical, mental, psychological, financial, coercive abuse who had agreed to participate through a research website which is now closed) were difficult to reach because their movements were controlled and most were subject to insecure immigration status, financial and language barriers. The author was mindful that the potential participants were not placed at additional risk by engaging in research and therefore participants who were receiving additional support services were selected.

Questions ranged from 1 to 20 and enabled an in-depth exploration of the participants' reasoning for selecting a particular forum, choosing different options of mediation and solutions, experiences under Islamic and English mediation, MIAM experiences, views on screening process under both forums, experiences as domestic abuse victims, type of Islamic solution/justice expected, English family courts approached and problems encountered, particularly relating to different sources of power imbalances within mediation among Muslim women choosing Shari'a Councils. In addition, reference was drawn to the Qur'anic verse Q.4:34 regarding how domestic abuse issue was treated by Shari'a Councils, particularly, but due to lack of space, this is not explored.

Focus Group

A focus group (Calder, 1977; Breen, 2006) of five women was used to gather feedback on using Islamic and English mediation and as victims of domestic abuse, how they were treated by religious scholars and English mediators and as victims of abuse, the type of justice expected, particularly justice based on egalitarian principles these women were seeking. Participants in the focus group contested that as victims of abuse the English law does not always deliver justice, particularly for those who are denied legal aid or do not have a legal immigration status in the UK including government organisations such as the Home Office.

The focus group consisted of diverse demographic characteristics and recorded separately. These women offered some valuable insights to seeking individualised, egalitarian justice and were not concerned about seeking justice from the English family justice system. The majority of the women considered seeking Islamic justice first and wanted to observe religious values. Of the five women from the focus group, all five were practising Muslims and seeking Islamic solutions based on egalitarian principles. The remaining two members of the focus group were concerned with an autonomous-based justice (what was important to each participant to achieve) from Islamic Councils but agreed with others that egalitarian principles should be applied.

Results and Findings

The primary data collected here is valuable as personal testimonies enrich our understanding of lived experience and law in action. Some interesting results emerged on Islamic plurality and spiritual loyalty towards egalitarian principles and these women defined this as 'gender-just' narratives based on classical female scholars such as A'isha Bint Abi Bakr (Prophet Muhammad's wife), 'egalitarian justice' defined in the Qur'an (Kadivar, 2013). Most participants provided a strong critique that Islamic arbitration and mediation offers greater justice if egalitarian principles are adopted. We can learn from narratives that make use of Shari'a Councils that these women seek to cultivate an ethical self by actively engaging with values, norms and codes of conduct they perceive as essential to the nurturing of their faith. They strive to take part in a moral universe in which Islam is the discursive terrain upon which believers collectively struggle to define alternative conceptions of justice. The abuse of 'religious authority' was something English law was deemed to safeguard women against as these are non-binding. South Asians and other Muslim women claimed to follow Islam observed by the early Muslims in Prophet Muhammad's time. There were 12 women in unregistered (religious-only) marriages, and this was higher than expected in the sample of 25 and were both British and immigrants. This also represents a vulnerability problem which the government is trying to address based on Law Commission's recommendations, 'Outdated weddings laws to be overhauled under new reforms'.[9] The recommendations are both timely and long overdue in the present circumstances, such as the pandemic rules allowing preliminaries and even the ceremonies itself to be carried out remotely. Therefore, reforms of the antiquated laws are required, for example, to the Marriage Act 1949.

Of the 25 women, 13 were British and in both civil and religious marriages; of the 13 British women, four were in polygamous religious-only marriages (these women's husbands had another religious wife). For example, one such woman was a successful family law solicitor with one child from her ten-year marriage and did not care what her husband did because she had a successful career. Of the 25 women, six were British women in religious-only marriages; 12 were immigrants and without valid leave and unable to marry legally and therefore, they were in religious-only marriages (only five were South Asian Muslims) who did not hold formal qualifications such as a degree. The 12 immigrants had entered the UK on student visa and this expired, visitor visa (seven women) and this expired and are remaining as over-stayers, immigrants entering with an agent at a UK port without a valid passport and claiming asylum (there were five women) and had exhausted all the appeal process. These women had entered the UK between 2012 and 2014. As these women did not have permission to stay in the UK, they were advised by solicitors, family friends and community friends that if they marry a settled or a British person then they can settle on human rights grounds or discretionary leave to remain under immigration rules, mainly Article 8 (right to private and family life). These women were aware that if they legally attempted to marry, then they face the possibility of being detained by immigration authorities and face removal.

Of the 25 women, four were in the UK on a spouse visa which had expired and did not have possession of their passports and/or their marriage certificates, they had validly entered the UK (spouse visa) with both civil and religious marriage ceremonies taking place abroad. All four had applied to the Home Office under domestic violence provision of the immigration rules.[10]

Of the 25 women, 17 considered egalitarian Islamic justice was fairer than the present system adopted by Shari'a Councils and they did not consider that the English family justice system treated them fairly. For example, immigrants have no access to legal aid or the justice system and there are no special interventions for Muslim victims of abuse because these women require different treatment to the non-Muslim victims who seek, for example, *fatwas* (religious rulings they abide) from local imams, Shari'a Councils and online. One common theme among the interviewees was that they all voluntarily approached Shari'a Councils because, of the 25 women, 17 wanted egalitarian justice (based on the Qur'an, *Sunna* and cited A'isha's (gender-just) narratives from *ahadith*, sayings of the Prophet). Participant one in the focus group said, 'we are Muslims and want a religious remedy based on "gender-just principles" (egalitarian justice) since the Qur'an was revealed to liberate the oppressed women, orphans and the poor'. The second participant said, 'religious remedy cannot be overlooked and therefore, English remedies are for those women in extreme violent marriages'. Women wanted to exercise their autonomy and choose egalitarian Islamic justice. These women had confirmed that migrant and gender discrimination also exist under the English justice system and only in the case of extreme violence would women resort to the police and the English family courts. These women appeared to be happy to use Shari'a Councils but suggested reforms to adopt the English mediation principles.

The five participants in the focus group were not referred to mediation but had attended MIAMs. Of the 25 women, 12 attended mediation and one of them said, 'mediators do not pick up on body language and they need to play an active interventionist role to remove power imbalances relating to finances', and the other 11 agreed. Of the 25 women, 10 confirmed that inequalities/injustices are greater for Muslim women and English mediators need specific or special training to deal with these cases (interviewed in 2016). There were also concerns raised about financial agreements where some English mediators did not request men to disclose financial evidence and unsatisfactory outcomes were reached. Women had very little confidence in English mediation and 16 women confirmed that there should be an Islamic mediator working with an English mediator (this would be a co-mediation model) to point out the financial rights of a wife particularly for an abused wife.

Situation One – Domestic Abuse and Mahr (Pre-nuptial Gift)

Sobia said:

> I felt that an Islamic mediator will understand issues from an Islamic perspective and not the English culture. I attended a simultaneous mediation session, but we were seen separately. My husband told me to apply for *khula* (divorce instigated by wife and she loses *mahr*) I just wanted my Islamic *mahr* but due to *khula* the religious mediator cited a verse of the Qur'an and told me that I lost my right for *mahr* even though I was forced to apply for *khula* (initiated by wife) as a consequence of violence.[11]

The above participant attended mediation and was referring to a single session. This participant was seen separately and to some extent this addressed to eliminate power imbalance. The main reason for divorce was 'domestic abuse' and the wife was pressured to apply for a divorce with mutual consent of her husband. However, this partic28ipant's bargaining position was compromised due to domestic abuse. There are three common divorces taking place at these Shari'a Councils, *talaq* (initiated by the husband and *mahr* is not required to be returned to the husband); *khula* (on mutual consent or known as nonfault divorce, wife instigates divorce and loses *mahr* or the husband can give up the return of the *mahr*) and *faskh* – instigated by the wife and obtained from a religious authority in the absence of the husband if he refuses to divorce her and *mahr* is retained, if paid at the time of marriage or not recoverable (Esposito and DeLong-Bas, 2001). The religious mediator did not attempt to correct this power imbalance relating to *mahr* and he should have recognised the fault of violence on the husband's part to advise the wife to retain her *mahr*. Religious sources were used to undermine the woman's right to *mahr* in a domestic abuse case. Mediated agreements arising from a climate of intimidation or violence involving two unequal parties was likely to produce an agreement that was neither just nor equitable (Astor, 1994).

Situation Two – Immigration Status and Lack of State Legal Aid Funding

Annie said:

> I was an overstayer (visa had expired) and I went to see several solicitors who said without legal aid they could not help me because I did not qualify due to my immigration status. I called one Islamic Shari'a Council and a female scholar told me she will assist me. I went to a joint mediation session and my husband was only prepared to give me one thousand pounds out of my 5,000 pounds *mahr* and my husband said I might be removed by the authorities as I am reporting to an immigration officer. I accepted one thousand to pay to legalise my immigration status.[12]

In this case, the Shari'a Council agrees to assist and told Annie to pay later and therefore filling the gap left by the English justice system. The immigration status of one party should not be used against the other. The mediator should have steered the direction of the negotiations to focus on making the full payment and at least a greater portion of the sum. The imbalance of power triggered by the immigration status weakened the bargaining position of the wife. As Islamic mediators have a greater interventionist role, he should have informed about other options such as referring the wife to a legal aid mediator, a solicitor and/or English family courts. In this case, the immigration was also used against her under English law as she was excluded from legal aid.

Empirical Evidence and Power Imbalances

A common theme among all interviewees approaching Shari'a Council was that they wanted to choose an egalitarian Islamic justice forum. This is different from some of the previous research carried out because Muslim women are seeking to resolve their disputes in accordance with what they believe to be following egalitarian (gender-just) Islamic principles and, therefore, approach Shari'a Councils for a female scholar.

Initial mediation sessions conducted were based on Islamic principles to avoid marriages breaking up and in the event of reconciliation failing to obtain a divorce. All five participants in the focus group raised the issue of risk assessment or screening process within Shari'a Councils to be improved and explored the possibility if English mediators and Shari'a Councils can work in partnership. Women aware of MIAMs felt that male scholars disregarded MIAM exemptions. Of the 25 women, 13 were asked to remain in the same room as the perpetrator (husband) in domestic abuse cases for an initial meeting. This has serious repercussions such as further harm to the victim, oppression and more sensitivity needs to be shown to such victims and the law. These types of sessions are likely to be counterproductive for women if the victim is made to feel uneasy or intimidated as it effectively continues the abuse in another way. In understanding women's narratives, and those of other participants cited above, it is important to place them in both their context of the focus group environment and its aims of participating in Islamic mediation, MIAMs and English mediation.

In relation to the five women in the focus group (all were interviewed in a group discussion on 1 July 2016), the first participant attended MIAM and was referred to the family court and she said, 'the reason why I attended an Islamic forum is because it is subtle and less intrusive'. For these women, individual justice prioritises over seeking remedies under the English family justice system. Another woman responded during the discussions that 'Islamic law does not always provide justice and discriminates against women whereas English family justice system is designed to protect women more' (participant two). The first participant responded and said,

> English family justice system can deny justice to women, for example, refuse legal aid, but with an Islamic system at least the scholars (if females) are willing to provide assistance and interpret rulings thorough A'isha's gender-just [egalitarian approach] (A'isha Bint Abi Bakr was Prophet Muhammad's wife).

It also revealed that these women prioritised individualised justice that complied with their religious beliefs.

Another participant argued that 'justice is at the core of the Qur'an and it adopts egalitarian values which are compatible with English law. The West has adopted many of the Islamic egalitarian values much later' (participant three). A participant responded and said,

> if we look at the example of A'isha then we can see how she applied 'gender just, treated fairly, to be respected equally' [egalitarian principles] to legal rulings and corrected male scholars such as Abu Hurayra (companion of Prophet Muhammad).
>
> (participant four)

One woman who had attended MIAM session told others that 'MIAM meeting is just a formality and it doesn't even bother to consider Muslim women's religious sensitivities. It is simply a process for ticking the boxes and pass you to the family court' (participant five). This means that Shari'a Councils are fulfilling a need that the family courts are not addressing. It was noted that women hesitated to approach the courts because they considered this to be the last resort and, even then, they wanted to avoid it.

Participants chose to address the patriarchal application of Islamic family law by retrieving the female religious authority characters in Islam such as A'isha Bint Abi Bakr, who applied egalitarian principles from Islam. Women are exercising their autonomy in different ways, not just choosing between an informal setting (Islamic) or a formal English mediation but seek to reform patriarchal Islamic practices adopted through their agency and voices. Islamic forum offers the opportunity for individualised justice which can provide a resolution to meet the needs of the parties, and those that are legally represented would be expected to know the relevant legal provisions and legal consequences of settlement options. However, litigants in person do not have this advantage.

Islamic forum provides an important service for Muslim women seeking an alternative to courts and English mediation. Muslim women prioritised Islamic options and individual outcomes. Female scholars were more conscious to observe English family law because they were able to empathise with the victims and where possible referred women to pursue their cases with English family courts/solicitors. Shari'a Councils are now semi-recognised by many scholars, practitioners and users as part of the informal justice system for the Muslim community (Bano, 2012). Shari'a Councils have a growing body of users and not just South Asian Muslims but diverse and heterogenous Muslims approaching them. Therefore, it may be best to reflect on the possible reforms that could make them more effective in delivering a compatible standard of justice within Shari'a Councils by working towards having either a solicitor on the panel or a co-mediation model.

Reforms: Assisting Muslim Women

Shari'a Councils in some cases discussed above conducted mandatory joint mediation to start divorce proceedings in domestic abuse cases resulting in power imbalances. There are many sources but, in this research, the following were discovered: domestic abuse, immigration status, financial situation, abuse of religious authority, litigants in person and inequalities. The state could support to make informal mediation into semi-formal mediation by encouraging the appointment of a legally qualified mediator or lawyer under English law to work in partnership with Shari'a Councils because this can help to identify power imbalances and maintain impartiality to assess whether mediation is a suitable forum. It would be more appropriate to have an integrated co-mediation model. This would involve an English and Islamic mediator working as co-mediators and adopting egalitarian principles within Islamic mediation.

This research seeks to establish trust across two scholarly traditions in order to propose a pilot model for the British context yet rooted in ethical Islamic thought compatible with English principles of law. This model will be based on the egalitarian methodology of A'isha Bint Abi Bakr (Prophet Muhammad's wife) to minimise power imbalances as it will seek to deliver gender justice and equality. The model will require four key principles to be adopted when mediating: dignity (Sachedina, 2009: 272), justice (Kadivar, 2013), equality (Mir-Hosseini, 2015) and equity (Smith, 1979) derived from the Qur'an which A'isha adopted in her approach (Geissinger, 2011). A'isha was not only an early legal scholar, she was the second largest *hadith* narrator and a jurist adopting this method and she taught many of the Prophet's companions egalitarian principles (meaning to remain faithful to sources) and she dealt with many gender issues arising in her time (Spellberg, 1994). These principles can be further developed to place a screening process for domestic abuse victims particularly with reference to egalitarian justice (Kadivar, 2013: 224) from the Qur'an by drawing on earlier judicial judgments in which legal rulings were given but it is beyond the scope of this chapter to explore this or A'isha's methodology (Rabb and Balbale, 2017). This can become compatible with English principles of mediation: voluntary participation, suitability, impartiality, confidentiality.[13]

Conclusion

The findings revealed new evidence relating to egalitarian framework to be used within Shari'a Councils (from the Qur'an, *Sunna* and A'isha's methodology) and on contested parts of women using Islamic and English mediation and there was very little redress available under the English family justice system. The new themes that emerged were: women chose Islamic forum despite the inequalities and power imbalances because the English courts cannot provide an Islamic divorce; women challenged patriarchy but advanced egalitarian narratives based on early classical female scholarship, particularly A'isha; women also were only willing to seek redress from courts in extreme violence cases and women suffered inequalities and power imbalances under English mediation. This represents a significant challenge for the family law field and one that failed to critically engage the related questions of mediating across cultural and religious differences.

The empirical evidence revealed that women can suffer under both systems as victims of domestic abuse and their freedom, autonomy and power can be compromised. The decision whether to opt for an informal or formal mediation forum or formal English family justice system is determined by risk of abuse, denial of legal aid and observance of religion, religious values and individual factors. The state can encourage safeguards and work closely with the Muslim community to improve the standard of justice delivered, procedural fairness, minimise power imbalances and eliminate gender inequality to reflect fairness within Shari'a Councils.

92 *Naheed Ghauri*

Notes

1 Domestic-Abuse-PD12J, https://www.judiciary.uk/wp-content/upload 2017/09/presidents-cicular-domestic-abuse-pd12j-substituted-pd-20170914.pdf accessed on 04.04.2021.
2 In 2018, 1.3 million women and 695,000 men experienced domestic abuse, https://www.gov.uk?government/publications/domestic-abuse-bill-2019-overaching-fact-sheet accessed on 06.11.2021.
3 Foucault (1982) identified three types of struggle: against domination on religious, ethnic and religious grounds.
4 FMC Code of Conduct, http://www.familymediationcouncil.org.uk/wp-content/uploads/2018/05/fmc-code-of-practice-may-2018.pdf accessed on 31.03.2021.
5 Home Office, Independent Review into Shari'a Law Launched (Home Office 2016), www.gov.uk/government/news/independent-review-into-shari'a-law-launched accessed 14.04. 2021.
6 See, Refah Partisi (The Welfare Party) and Others v Turkey (No 1) (2002) 35 EEHR 3 at [72].
7 FMC Code of Conduct, n 4.
8 Birkbeck Ethics Research Guidelines, http://www.bbk.ac.uk/committees/research-integrity/guidelinesresearchwiththeethicalImplications.pdf accessed on 20.06.2012.
9 'Outdated Weddings Laws to Be Overhauled under New Reforms', https://www.lawcom.gov.uk/centuries-old-weddings-laws-to-be-overhauled-under-new-reforms/ accessed 27.08.2022.
10 Immigration Rules: Victims of Domestic Violence, Appendix FM (Section DVILR-E-DVILR), http://www.gov.uk/guidance/immigration-rules/immigration-rules-appendix-fm-family-members accessed 13.03.2021.
11 Interviewed on 1 July 2016.
12 Interviewed on 20 July 2016.
13 FMC Code of Conduct, n 6.

Bibliography

Abdalla, A., (2001) 'Principles of Islamic Interpersonal Conflict Intervention: A Search within Islam and Western Literature', *Journal of Law and Religion*, Vol 15, No 1, 151–84.
Astor, H., (1994) 'Violence and Family Mediation Policy', *Australian Journal of Family Law*, Vol 8, 3–21.
Bano, S., (2012) *Muslim Women and Shari'ah Councils Transcending the Boundaries of Community and Law*, London: Palgrave Macmillan.
Breen, R. L., (2006) A Practical Guide to Focus-Group Research, *Journal of Geography in Higher Education*, Vol 30, No 3, 463–75.
Brigg, M., (2008) *The New Politics of Conflict Resolution*, London: Palgrave Macmillan.
Calder, B. J., (1977) 'Focus Groups and the Nature of Qualitative Marketing Research', *Journal of Marketing Research*, Vol 14, No 3, 353–64.

Esposito, J. and DeLong-Bas, N. J., (2001) *Women in Muslim Family Law*, Syracuse, NY: Syracuse University Press.

Foucault, M., (1982) 'The Subject and Power', *Critical Inquiry*, Vol 8, No 4, 777–95.

Gee, J. P. and Handford, M., (2013) *The Routledge Handbook of Discourse Analysis*, London: Routledge.

Geissinger, A., (2011) 'A'isha Bint Abi Bakr and Her Contributions to the Formation of the Islamic Tradition', *Religion Compass*, Vol 5, No 1, 37–49.

Glaser, B. G. and Strauss, A. L., (1967) *The Discovery of Grounded Theory: Strategies for Qualitative Research*, Chicago, IL: Aldine.

Griffith-Jones, R., (2013) 'The 'Unavoidable' Adoption of Shari'a Law – The Generation of a Media Storm', In: R Griffith-Jones (ed.) *Islam and English Law – Rights and Responsibilities and the Place of Shari'a*, Cambridge: Cambridge University Press, 9–19.

Hesse-Biber, S. N. and Leavy, P., (2006) *The Practice of Qualitative Research*, London: Sage Publications.

Hester, M. and Pearson, C., (1997) 'Domestic Violence and Mediation Practices: A Summary of Recent Research Findings', *Family Mediation*, Vol 7, No 1, 10.

Hirschmann, N. J., (2013) 'Freedom, Power and Agency in Feminist Legal Theory', In: M. Davies and V. E. Munro (eds.) *The Ashgate Research Companion to Feminist Legal Theory*, Farnham: Ashgate, 51–64.

Kadivar, M., (2013) 'Revisiting Women's Rights in Islam – 'Egalitarian Justice' in Lieu of 'Dessert-based Justice'', In: Z. Mir-Hosseini, K. Vogt, L. Larsen and C. Moe (eds.) *Gender and Equality in Muslim Family Law – Justice and Ethics in the Islamic Legal Tradition*, London: I.B. Tauris, 213–33.

Maclean, M. and Eekelaar, J., (2016) *Lawyers and Mediators the Brave New World of Services for Separating Families*, Bloomsbury: Hart.

Manea, E., (2016) *Women and Shari'a Law - The Impact of Legal Pluralism in the UK*, London: I.B. Tauris.

Mir-Hosseini, Z., (2015) 'Muslim Legal Tradition and the Challenge of Gender Equality', In: Z Mir-Hosseini, M Al-Sharmani and J Rumminger (eds.) *Men in Charge? Rethinking Authority in Muslim Legal Tradition*, London: One world Publications, 13–43.

Okin, S. M., (1999) 'Is Multiculturalism Bad for Women?', In: S. M. Okin, J. Cohen, M. Howard and M. C. Nussbaum (eds.) *Is Multiculturalism Bad for Women?* Princeton, NJ: Princeton University Press, 1st edition.

Rabb, I and Balbale, (2017) A K, *Justice and Leadership in Early Islamic Courts*, Cambridge: Islamic Legal Studies Program, Harvard Law School.

Sachedina, A., (2009) *Islam and the Challenge of Human Rights*, New York: Oxford University Press.

Smith, J., (1979) 'Women in Islam: Equity, Equality, and the Search for the Natural Order', *Journal of the American Academy of Religion*, Vol 47, No 4, 517–37.

Spellberg, D. A., (1994) *The Legacy of A'isha Bint Abi Bakr*, New York: Columbia University Press.

Walker, L. E. A., (2016) *The Battered Women Syndrome*, New York: Springer Publishing Company, 4th edition.

Webley, L., (2017) 'When Is Mediation Mediatory and When Is It Really Adjudicatory? Religion, Norms, and Decision Making', In: S. Bano (ed) *Gender and Justice in Family Law Disputes: Women, Mediation and Religious Arbitration*, Waltham MA and New England: Brandeis University Press, 25–45.

5 Sharia Councils and Muslim Family Law

Analysing the Parity Governance Model, the Sharia Inquiry and the Role of the State/Law Relations

Samia Bano

Introduction

Drawing upon critical legal and feminist scholarship this chapter evaluates the Sharia Inquiry findings and analyses the possible value and/or potential limitations of the 'parity governance' model (broadly conceived as gender parity) to be constitutively applied as a framework of 'democratic governance' to Muslim legal pluralist models of dispute resolution (identified as Sharia Councils and the Muslim Arbitration Tribunal).

Multiculturalism and its normative concern for justice, equality and fairness have of course long been debated, theorized, critiqued and challenged. The twin goals of the 'accommodation' of cultural and religious differences and practices and the limits of such 'recognition' have led to the emergence of a renewed liberal political discourse and public policy development(s) dealing with the specific conflicts of 'minority rights', individual rights versus group rights and the tensions created by different sets of obligations owed to self, family, community and state law. Political and social theorists have, for example, long traced the European liberal legal tradition of 'minority rights' with a focus on problems generated by conflicting of norms and normativity (social and legal/state law norms) and the extent to which individuals are able to choose between two or more sets of conflicting norms in the face of group loyalty versus state law obligations.

The chapter raises a set of related questions. Firstly, a closer analysis on the institutional design of private community governance in Britain identified as Sharia Councils and the Muslim Arbitration Tribunal: what is it about these bodies that signifies 'Islam', 'Muslim practice' and 'Muslimness'? How are these bodies conceptualized in

DOI: 10.4324/9781003090410-6

relation to ideas of liberal justice, human rights and equality? What are the contours of the debates and the resolution of family law disputes within the processes of what we understand as dispute resolution? Can we capture an assertion of Muslim subjectivity and Muslim autonomy in these spaces? And does this assertion of Muslim subjectivity undermine state law legal processes?

The diverse, contested and varied experiences of South Asian Muslim women utilizing unofficial dispute resolution mechanisms such as Sharia Councils and more formalized religious bodies such as the Muslim Arbitration Tribunal are increasingly being documented and demonstrate the ways in which debates on belonging, identity and rights cannot be understood as fixed and unchanging.[1] Debates across UK and Europe have focused on policies of multiculturalism and the extent to which minority religious practices are tolerated and/or endorsed by national domestic courts. Further afield debates in Canada, US and increasingly Australia highlight issues of conflict, equity and discrimination. Muslim women remain at the centre of these debates while feminists from across the political spectrum seek to defend or resist calls for greater accommodation of religious norms and values and practices in Western democratic societies. This has led to enormous conflicts, crossing political spectrums and the extent to which state law should recognize alternative systems of family law dispute resolution. As Marie Ashe and Anissa Helie explain,

> Civil governmental recognitions of jurisdiction in specifically-religious courts may be the most extraordinary of the accommodations currently being provided to religious organisations. The toleration of judicial autonomy in such bodies in itself manifests a striking sharing of sovereignty. And the ceding to religious bodies of a central feature of governmental sovereignty – the judicial power – becomes particularly problematic when that power is utilized in order to enforce religious law that conflicts with fundamental principles of the civil law.[2]

Debates have therefore focused on the extent to which religious legal practices comply with liberal legalism and gender equality raising a further set of questions: Do such bodies discriminate against Muslim women? Are women's rights, liberty and equality under threat? Is justice being administered in the shadow of the law? The controversy of Sharia, it seems, will not only not disappear but is increasing in its intensity and vigour both by its opponents and its supporters. This raises the important question raised again by Ashe and Helie as to whether such bodies should be tolerated at all. Can the 'problem' in fact be resolved? 'The non-settled status of sharia-related questions', they argue, 'invites broader more historically-informed, and more comparative inquiry concerning the policies that should shape liberal-governmental interaction with religious courts in general'.[3] Why, for example, under a liberal multiculturalist framework is the demand for religious and communal group autonomy considered both inevitable and necessary rather than questioning the basis upon which demands are made and met?

In Britain, new methods of dispute resolution in English family law have also led to an unprecedented rise in the number of scholarly and policy critiques questioning their effectiveness and the challenge to liberal legal principles of 'equality before the law', 'justice' and 'common citizenship'.[4] Debates have focused on the wider discussions of promoting 'access to justice' for all citizens and to better understand the relationship between cultural and social norms that may underpin new forms of dispute resolution. Indeed the contemporary landscape of civil and family justice in England and Wales is part of a renewed recognition by the state to build upon mechanisms of Alternate Dispute Resolution (ADR) that are evidenced by the increasing use of arbitration, mediation, conciliation and initiatives developed by practitioners such as collaborative law. As part of these contemporary developments, issues of cultural and religious diversity are addressed including demands for the accommodation of religious dispute mechanisms as part of new dispute resolution initiatives. We have seen, for example, a rise in cross-cultural mediation mechanisms in determining both the use and delivery of services and the desire to accommodate the needs of all users, irrespective of cultural and religious differences. In essence, what we see then is not only the emergence of new forms of legal cultures but also the ways in which new forms of informal and formal adjudication in all their complexity emerge and develop within groups, communities and networks.

The Sharia Inquiry Findings: Brief Overview

The independent review into Sharia Law in England and Wales was tasked to examine the practice of Islamic law in England and Wales with a specific focus on the potential mis-abuse of Sharia Councils in their position as alternative dispute resolution fora within Muslim communities. The focus was on Sharia Councils therefore and not sharia practices in general. A public call for evidence was issued and this led to a wide range of evidence being collated including users of

Sharia Councils, women's rights groups, academics and lawyers and other key stakeholders. A Sharia Council was defined as 'a voluntary local association of scholars who see themselves or are seen by their communities as authorised to offer advice to Muslims principally in the field of religious marriage and divorce'.

Key findings included: (i) the primary users of Sharia Councils are women; (ii) the primary motivation was due to the fact that Muslim couples do not register their marriages and therefore some Muslim women have no option of obtaining a civil divorce; (iii) evidence of good and bad practice was found. The panel put forward a set of recommendations including changing the marriage laws in England and Wales to ensure Muslim marriages fall under the remit of registered marriages. Further an awareness campaign was conducted within Muslim communities to educate and inform women of their rights under English law. There was also a partial call of regulation to Sharia Councils but this was not supported by all panel members and the regulation comprised a state-mandated self-regulatory body.

Multiculturalism and Managing Migrant Communities

Debates on the nature and settlement of postcolonial migrations are often discussed in relation to discussions on identity, ethnicity, religion, migration and the impact of transnational populations upon settled communities. Within a wide body of scholarship and sociological research we are better able to understand how notions of diaspora, hybridity and globalism intersect with social and class divisions, gender, ethnicity and class. Today, therefore, there is a growing literature which seeks to understand identities as multiple, fluid, dynamic and partial and which can only be understood in interaction with other identities, ethnicities and social structures. This understanding of identity as fluid and changing has led many commentators to conclude that, at specific times, a particular aspect of the group identity emerges. In Britain, for example, we have seen the emergence of a 'renewed' Muslim religious identity as part of South Asian Muslim communities[5] and demands for the accommodation of religious systems of law to be made under this understanding of identity.

The term 'multiculturalism' in Britain today is debated, discussed, contested, challenged and more recently dismissed. Indeed some of the problems attributed to multiculturalism including the perceived lack of integration of minority ethnic communities into British society, the emergence of parallel and segregated minority ethnic communities and the failure to foster a national British identity only illustrates the shifts and contradictions in its meaning and what it was originally perceived to stand for. Current public commentary therefore pays much more attention to its perceived principal failure rather than any real success. Whether the term has any epistemological value is itself open to question as are questions on measurable outcomes. At its best, multiculturalism promotes tolerance, equality and respect for cultural and religious difference, promoting positive relations between minority and majority communities, but at its worst it promotes segregated, polarized and parallel communities who have little care or understanding how the 'other' may live. For many it is this politics of difference and the threshold of tolerance that remain problematic; for example, at which point does a cultural practice become intolerant and oppressive and to whom? For many liberal multiculturalists the threshold is to protect vulnerable members within communities and in Muslim communities this has often meant Muslim women being protected against what is often deemed oppressive, archaic and traditional religious practices. In other words, the principles of freedom and choice are seen as easily compromised in Muslim communities where the protection of Muslim women becomes the benchmark upon which we must fight for women's rights and liberal values of freedom, justice and equality. In her work Lila Abu-Lughod warns of the dangers this can bring, explaining that

> ... generalizing about cultures prevents us from appreciating or even accounting for people's experiences and the contingencies with which we all live. The idea of culture increasingly has become a core component of international politics and common sense. Pundits tell us that there is a clash of civilizations or cultures in our world. They tell us there is an unbridgeable chasm between the West and the 'Rest'. Muslims are presented as a special and threatening culture – the most homogenized and the most troubling of the Rest. Muslim women in this new common sense, symbolize just how alien this culture is.[6]

Today, in an age where the practice and discourse of multiculturalism and policies of diversity and managing diversity is coming under increasing attack from all sides of the political spectrum, questions of culture (whose culture?) and rights (whose rights?) become ever more urgent in the context of the settlement and management of minority ethnic and religious groups in Western democratic societies.

The twin policies of social cohesion and integration has led to what Patel (2008) identifies as a move away from multiculturalism and towards what she describes as 'multi-faithism', with government policies specifically promoting and nurturing 'faith communities'. For Patel the encroaching of secular spaces that are increasingly being taken up by religious groups means that women from minority backgrounds are left with even less choice. She explains,

> Ironically, the current promotion of faith based projects in all areas of civil society will compromise the gender equality agenda for black and minority women in particular. It will divert women away from the legal justice system into the hands of religious conservative and fundamentalist leaders. The cry of religious discrimination can and will be used to claim access to and control over resources, whilst at the same time it will serve to perpetuate discrimination against women and other sub groups and to deter state intervention in family matters.[7]

Not only does this lead to a denial of rights for women from minority ethnic backgrounds but this critique also flags up central questions of power, voice and representation and the use of male interlocutors in forging majority/minority relations between communities and the state. Further critique points to an outcome for minority ethnic communities who may feel disempowered from processes of power but the focus on cultural and religious difference that has in fact led to a form of limited autonomy over internal 'community' affairs, such as religious observance, dress and food. In other words the emphasis upon communities to focus on their culture and religion has in effect led to a shift away from public decision-making spaces. More worrying however it has also led to the emergence of community leaders who often have the undemocratic mandate to represent their communities. For example, male leaders, over time, have become the primary interlocutors and are afforded the right to speak on behalf of the whole community and are seen as both legitimate and with authority. Women are in effect then side-lined and given less voice and capacity to engage with community and state practices.

Islam and the 'Muslim Question'

The 'Muslim Question' (generated by a series of questions over integration/loyalty to the state/citizenship and claims for religious communal autonomy in family law matters, to name but a few) has, in recent times, come to be understood (by scholars and policy makers alike) as one of *the* defining questions in the twenty-first century when framing, challenging and debating issues ranging from the limits of liberal free speech, minority rights, questions of modernity, immigration, liberalism, multiculturalism and most importantly, of course, issues of gender equality, injustice and personal autonomy for potentially vulnerable Muslim women living within Muslim families and communities. This literature is accompanied by an expansive body of scholarship tracing the social and lived realities of Muslim communities in the UK,[8] rights of minority communities and multiculturalism,[9] to charting the rise of anti-Muslim discrimination and 'Islamophobia'[10] and tracing the rise of religious intolerance and the emergence of a politics of fear and the limits of anti-discrimination legislation. Furthermore it seems that the 'Muslim Problem' is inextricably linked to the 'Secularism Problem' with the juxtaposition of religion and secularism and the public and private spheres deemed imaginary, problematic and illusory. For example, the works of Saba Mahmood[11] (2012), Talal Asad[12] (2011), Oliver Roy[13] (2010) and Salman Sayyid[14] (2014) demonstrate *how* debates on secularism are closely linked to the ways in which Muslim mobilizations in the West are managed, controlled and designated in western European societies often through security and racist governmentalities. In Britain, for example, the government's Prevent strategy has been critiqued for not only the loss of civil liberties but its focus on Muslim communities and the potential consequences that this kind of exceptionalism promotes. This body of literature raises important questions regarding the separation of religious and political spaces in liberal politics and the junctures upon which religious personal practices can be located and accommodated as part of the liberal human rights framework. As Sayyid points out, 'secularism is one of the categories often deployed in discussions about the difficulties of exercising Muslim agency'.[15] Therefore, what are the dialogic processes and challenges between community and state law relations if Muslim communities seek not to operate from a liberal legal and ethical framework? What are the other possibilities for communicative or intercultural dialogue(s)? Are minority Muslim communities in Europe simply in need of secularization?

Critiques on liberal legal models aim therefore to de-centre the 'West' and challenge the 'Western imaginary' as *the* dominant loci of politics, governance and identity. Indeed the contemporary binary oppositions of Islam and the West are not only widely acknowledged as a reflection of the hegemony of Western legal liberalism but the framing and naming of Islam and Muslim legal pluralism has led to disjunctures between 'official laws' and 'law as a lived social reality'. Questions of 'norms', 'truth' and claims-making have focused on the uneasy tensions produced by communities with liberal and democratic principles of liberal legal conceptions of justice, equality before the law, human rights and citizenship. The focus on Islam and Muslims remains important for both communities and state law relations because 'the act of naming is also the act of becoming'.[16] In other words the ways in which Muslims name themselves as Muslims and construct *ways* of belonging (for example, belonging to the Muslim community or the Muslim Ummah) coupled with the ways in which communities are understood (or imagined) in non-Muslim societies contributes to policy initiatives and community-state relations. Furthermore the ways in which Muslim communities 'imagine' the Muslim Ummah can help our conceptualizations of community and Muslim autonomy. Therefore the rubric upon which we frame debates can also help to reframe debates on cultural and religious autonomy and finding legal remedies to protect vulnerable members of communities subject to religious personal systems of law, most often Muslim women.

Indeed this act of becoming as taken shape and form in a myriad of ways as epitomized by the emergence of local grassroots Muslim community groups (including private community governance) and the different levels of state funding and state support. Over the past three decades, for example, we have seen the emergence of local Muslim women's groups, refuges and counselling services to the setting up of national organizations such as the Muslim Council of Britain[17] and the Muslim Women's Network[18] and numerous Sharia Councils and the Muslim Arbitration Tribunal.[19] The 2011 Census identified Islam as the second largest religion in the UK with a population of 2,786,635 and 4.4% of the total population. This act of becoming has therefore taken shape, for example, under the rubric of multiculturalism, policies of integration, socio-economic factors vis-à-vis community, state and cultural interlocutors. So what are the cultural impacts of these new formations in our understandings of Islam and Muslims living in non-Muslim-majority societies? What does the description of a 'Muslim community' mean for Muslims and non-Muslims alike? What are the processes of governance and governmentality that *signify* Muslim communities? And how can we conceptualize, identify and address issues of cultural inter- and intra-community conflicts addressing issues of unequal gender relations without relying on reified notions of culture, religion, belonging, identity and law?

Muslims and the Problem with Democracy?

In their article Ruiz and Rubio-Marin (2009)[20] point out that democratic parity 'must define what democracy is fundamentally about'. Similarly in her work Ann Philips[21] concludes that, 'Democratic parity matters because without it we do not yet have democracy'. While we also learn that this model 'has its own distinctive logic' such observations clearly point to an implicit relationship between the two, leading to some kind of normative conception of democracy. Of course all claims about meaning and value of concepts such as democracy merit scrutiny and both scholars successfully draw upon a political theory of democracy that promotes gender equality in ways that aim to avoid the pitfalls of essentialism and normative truth/claims-making as theorizing choice, capability and capacity from a feminist perspective. Feminist political theorists and philosophers have also (over the past two decades) developed new models to challenge discrimination and oppression occurring within particular cultural and religious settings (for example, Shachar[22] and her model of transformative accommodation).

In this part of the chapter, I pose a series of questions to consider the ways in which the idea and meaning of democracy as a common *signifier* of democracy may serve to ascribe meanings and value (within minority Muslim communities) in fixed and problematic ways. For example, the assumptions and goals of democracy; the way in which it engages and intersects with non-state norms and minority communities, while raising a critical reading on the relationship between democracy, the West and Islam. Our efforts to complicate the concepts and practice of democracy are important if democracy also exhibits an ensemble of practices and democratic institutions that seek to regulate the exercise of communal and private governance based upon orientalist tropes of Muslims simply lacking the credentials of freedom and democracy. The meaning, relevance and perils of democracy therefore raise important questions and challenges. For example, in his work on governmentality Foucault[23] poses a series of questions relating to the problems of government and the role of individuals. How should 'we govern oneself, how to be governed, by whom should we accept to be governed and how to be the best possible governor'? This series of lectures reveals important insights into the intricate and complex relationships between governance and the process of governing and the ways in which governance is both 'thought' and 'practised' by the liberal political processes. Governmentality he argues is in evidence across multiple sites (such as population) where technologies operate to regulate conduct and behaviours in ever complex ways displaying the myriad and multiple forms of political power in action. The multiple dynamics of power seek to define/address/manage and control with implications for all in minority and majority communities. Social and legal norms operate within and across communities in relation 'to the division of labour, authority between family members and intimate behaviour'. We have, of course, a long and expansive body of postcolonial scholarship that produces important insights into relations of power, legality and identity.

Yet even this (brief) overview of governmentality, power and state law relations raises important questions in relation to relations of power, dialogue, intercultural dialogue, positionality and rights and contributes to our understanding of the myriad and complex lived social realities of law and legalities that take shape in many different forms both in state law relations and as private governance within minority communities. The rise of racist governmentalities, for example, also raises an important set of questions as the logic of democracy that can also rest upon a logic of West and non-West and those who are democratic versus non-democratic. One could, for example, question upon what basis the *idea* of democracy is predicated in its application to minority Muslim communities living in Western societies? Western exceptionality and a fixed description of democracy (and democratic discourse) reveals a tenuous relationship between ideas of belonging, identity and a convergence of being democratic and being Western. Postcolonial critiques, for example, point to the Western hegemony and a fixed Western identity as the primary signifiers of democracy, today. So how can we better understand the category of democracy as it applies to Muslim communities? These critiques remain important for the dislocation within Muslim communities from ideas of citizenship, democracy and belonging is in evidence and raises a series of questions: what are the primary features of democracy and how can we understand questions of autonomous individuals, decision-making and capacity in relation to Muslim women and religious models of dispute resolution? What is the capacity of Muslim dispute resolution bodies to transform to accommodate 'difference within difference'? How do these organizations envisage democratic arrangements and governance? Are we able to produce alternative accounts both as insiders and outsiders of communities and groups? It is imperative, of course, that we unpack this *idea* of a Muslim community as the Muslim Ummah. As Sayyid points out, 'The Muslim question encompasses the difficulties associated with the emergence of a distinct political identity that appears to

be transgressive of the norms, conventions and structures that underpin the contemporary world.'[24] Yet surprising perhaps, in a world of
difference, complexity and challenge the emergence of fixed notions
of identity and religious has only in recent times gained increasing
urgency. Furthermore as a political signifier democracy with its particular cultural formations in the 'West' provides the essence of human identity transcending cultural and religious divides and acting
as a designator of freedom, capacity but also government practices
and hybrid Western identities. We therefore understand democracy
as closely aligned to a Western identity and to be anti-Western is to
be anti-democratic.

Institutional Design of Muslim Dispute Resolution Mechanisms

An analysis of the institutional design and power relations embedded
within Sharia Councils is of fundamental importance in order to consider the ways in which these bodies, today, are not only increasingly
understood as the primary expression of 'Muslim legal pluralism' but
also in order to consider the possible ways in which the 'parity governance' model may be useful in the process of the internal reform. All
such bodies are of course plural, that is, they are constructed around
multiple and often conflicting schools of thought, and the boundaries upon which they operate are constructed and depend upon a vast
number of social and religious rules and norms. More importantly
such rules, principles, procedures and sources are structured by a
whole host of factors including religious, ethnic, gender and class differences. The rule-making capacity of such bodies maybe relational
and specific to local contingencies but is also dependent upon certain
shared cultural and religious attributes that attribute identity and the
boundaries of such alternative dispute resolution mechanisms to the
authority of the religious scholar(s). In the case of Sharia Councils
important questions remain in relation to what kinds of structures
are created and what types of communication take place between the
sources of authority, religious scholars and primary users, most often Muslim women. Furthermore in what ways do principles of justice, rights and gender equality differ from liberal values and how
do such bodies operate as decision-making processes? What is the
institutional design and the constitutive elements in the operation of
justice? And does this system of dispute resolution recognize its own
contingencies? In other words is it even possible to have gender parity
in Sharia Councils and religious tribunals?

Democracy and equality remain the two foundational principles of the parity governance model with gender representation at its core. Conversely, the model of dispute resolution dominant in contemporary British Sharia Councils remains grounded in normative Islamic principles that render gender differentiated rights and duties and are marked by contested concepts of Islamic jurisprudential schools of thought. Therefore, there is an obvious challenge to the application of a parity design model upon these bodies, but if these challenges can be overcome what are the options for parity design as a process of reform within these bodies? In this part of the chapter I discuss the normative desirability or change in the institutional design or formal structure of these bodies but also focus on the ambiguous and contested concepts of religion that underpin these bodies. Parity claims, first and foremost, provide female members with exercising their rights within a liberal and egalitarian public culture. It strongly maintains that the equal representation of women is central to ensuring that liberal societies properly invoke the principles of democracy and equality. Women members from minority groups often pay a high cost if they are denied exercising their rights that are bestowed upon all citizens.

The history of Sharia Councils has been widely documented in Britain and can be traced to a diverse set of social, political and religious developments in civil society and as part of the emergence of a Muslim identity both forged and as part of multicultural practices. The question of how such bodies should be classified and understood, for example, as groups, associations, institutions or alternative dispute resolution mechanisms often rests upon the way they may operate and the nature of their relationship to multicultural practices and internal rules of process, institution, whether they rely on a hierarchal relationship and the structures and processes of decision-making and methods of enforcement. Moreover over the past three decades, a growing number of scholars have explored the changing and contested nature of this relationship, revealing a new discursive space of engagement, contestation and negotiation between minority religious communities and the state. This would include, for example, the emergence of Sharia Councils as part of mosques and religious community centres, more specifically in Britain charting from the past four decades. While these bodies can be identified as being autonomous and constructed by the institutional autonomy and frameworks of local religious loyalties and Islamic schools of thought many may actively seek to avoid any interaction with each other and any possible conflict with a secular state and civil law. In other words, such bodies exist also to distinguish themselves from other religious groups and religious practices to emerge as offering a very specific type of expertise.

Therefore to understand the emergence of Sharia Councils in Britain we need to begin, not with an overview of how they may function but the ways in which they have emerged as part of multicultural Britain and the recognition of cultural and religious practices as part of British Muslim lives. They are part of British Muslim communities that have established very specific ways in which family law disputes are resolved, yet there is on-going debate within British Muslim communities regarding their role, identity and future. There are complex variations and permutations of sharia councils as they are neither unified nor represent a single school of thought but instead are made up of various different bodies representing the different schools of thought in Islam and ethnic religious groups.

Debate on the emergence of Sharia Councils has largely been discussed and scrutinized in relation to debates on liberal multiculturalism and its limits on minority group rights. There is no single and authoritative definition of the term 'Sharia council' and therefore no obvious consensus on the role of these bodies within British Muslim communities. In essence, a Sharia Council has three key functions: issuing Muslim divorce certificates, reconciling and mediating between parties and producing expert opinion reports on matters of Muslim family law and custom to the Muslim community, solicitors and the courts. Existing scholarship, for example, provides little insight into the nature of rules within these bodies as institutionalized systems of dispute resolution. Concern in particular has focused on the rights and autonomy of minority group members and the potential conflicts generated by minority community norms and values in conflict with majority group norms and culture. Hegemonic relations of state law are understood as oppressive and over-bearing while undermining individual members' sense of belonging and autonomy as part of their faith communities. Protection of the individual vis-à-vis the group therefore has become imperative to the liberal project. However, as Karayanni[25] points out,

> as this theory of group rights crystallised, a major problem arose: how should liberal multiculturalism relate to religious minority groups that adhere to practices viewed as illiberal, for which they seek accommodation – in the form of jurisdictional autonomy over their members in matters of family law, recognition of their dress codes, absolution from criminal liability when they perform certain religiously motivated activities or other judicial leniencies?

This body of work challenges both the essentialism and uniformity assumed in state law relations and celebrates cultural and religious difference as demonstrative of the emerging parallel systems of law operating in British society. More specifically it contributes to our understanding of how contemporary societies are 'increasingly confronted within minority groups demanding recognition of their ethnicity and accommodation of their cultural and religious differences'. However, this literature also adopts a somewhat legal prescriptive analysis to understanding of the emergence of Sharia Councils and their relationship with and in opposition to state law. In short, there is little substantive and empirical analysis on the internal dynamics of power within these mechanisms of dispute resolution. Conceptualizing unofficial dispute resolution in this way is premised on the idea of homogeneity within 'Muslim communities' with little explanation on how these bodies are constituted within local communities. Furthermore, the primacy of a Muslim identity means that little is learnt about cultural and religious practices that may affect the autonomy of women using these bodies and how such processes are contested, redefined and used strategically to serve particular ends. Existing literature does not, for example, give due salience to the interconnection between the Sharia Councils, forms of power and gender inequality.

At present the nature and scope of Sharia Council activity in England and Wales remains largely unknown and undocumented. However, both the Sharia and Inquiry and a report by the Ministry of Justice entitled *An exploratory study of Shari'ah councils in England with respect to family law* identified 30 councils that worked on issues of Muslim family law and issued Muslim divorce certificates. Although this project did not look at smaller Sharia councils it suggests a relatively small number of key councils operating in England. The project found much diversity in the size of the councils, in the number of religious scholars providing advice and assistance, and in the composition of council members. Most councils were embedded within Muslim communities, forming part of mosques and community centres and appear to have evolved according to the needs of the communities in which they are located.

Another example of Muslim legal pluralism is the Muslim Arbitration Tribunal (MAT) that was set up in June 2007 and aims to settle disputes in accordance with religious Sharia Law. The authority of this tribunal rests with the Arbitration Act 1996 which permits civil matters to be resolved in accordance with Muslim law and within the ambit of state law. For many, this process of resolving disputes may provide the ideal forum that allows the arbitrating parties to resolve disputes according to English law while fulfilling any obligations under Islamic law. The advantages of arbitration, it is argued, allow the parties to achieve some level of autonomy in the decision-making process. This, coupled with the informal setting, lower costs, flexibility and time efficiency, means that for some it may prove a more attractive alternative to the adversarial courts system in England and Wales. However, there remain real concerns over whether this process can restrict women's equality and over issues of fairness and justice in family law.

Democratizing Muslim Legal Pluralism? Parity and Muslim Dispute Resolution

In an earlier part of this chapter I explored the problems of 'democracy' and what has been described as an emergence of forms of Muslim exceptionalism whereby liberal governance specifically targets Muslim communities. In this part of the chapter I question whether the Parity Democracy Model offers insights into the ways in which these processes of dispute resolution can promote gender parity in family law disputes. Empirical research on Sharia Councils suggests that the boundaries of community groups are often closed with a form of 'operative closure' that operates selectively and exclusively to reproduce norms that promote the closing of boundaries. We also know that this can lead to intra-cultural gender inequalities as this process can allow dispute resolution to evolve from a system of personal decision-making to one of oppressive norms and the application of sanctions including the loss of personal decision-making and the normative values upon which the process is based. While the rationale for applying a parity governance model upon community dispute resolution processes maybe questioned, nevertheless, it raises important questions on the ability of such a model to provide a framework to the administration and functioning of these types of councils. As Ziegert points out, 'The impossibility of communication *between* systems but the apparent historically varied correlations between the legal system and various other social systems require a more accurate observation as to how such relationships become possible and what form they take.'[26] There is now an important body of work which explores the liberal basis upon which religious and cultural autonomy may be recognized and accommodated in English law. Attempting to create new forms of accommodation, however, also raises questions of power and the extent to which minority groups rely on the political system to supply a normative framework for the political system's operations.

In his work, Eekelaar puts forward a model he describes as 'cultural voluntarism' which would allow individuals to continue following group norms as long as they comply with civil law norms.[27] He explains:

> family courts could make orders based on agreements reached under religious law but only if the agreement was genuine and followed independent advice, and was consistent with overriding policy goals (for example the best interests of the child). State law would be available at all times to anyone who chose to invoke it and access to it should be safeguarded and encouraged.[28]

Drawing upon this work, Malik[29] describes the emergence of 'minority legal order(s)' in Britain, defined around two key aspects: 'first, by its distinct cultural or religious norms; second, by some "systemic" features that allow us to say that there is a distinct institutional system for the identification, interpretation and enforcement of these norms'. This can be identified as Sharia Councils and other forms of Muslim dispute resolution processes. Malik puts forward a number of democratic participatory models that would allow both systems to operate with in-built democratic processes to deal with potential conflicts and tensions but also concludes that although there are good reasons to encourage cooperation between the state and minority legal orders, this cannot be implemented until further research is conducted to deal with how issues of justice and access to justice are addressed.[30] Again the concern is how to ensure the vulnerable members within groups are given adequate protection and safeguards.

Yet the question over the norms that act as the foundational bases upon which Muslim legal pluralism rests and the extent to which these forms can be tested, challenged and transformed is left largely unaddressed by both Eekelaar and Malik. While recognizing the problem of power and power relations in relation to norm-making whereby norms may be imposed by persons or elites within communities in order to advance their own interests or ideologies under the guise of the interests of the community, they do not offer an adequate response to how this problem can be overcome. While scholarship, therefore, considers the effects of religious accommodation in terms of the nature and extent to which this is practised within Muslim communities we also need to think through carefully the consequences for all members of communities including minorities within minority groups before a model of Muslim dispute resolution based upon the foundational principles of democracy and rights is adopted. What exactly is the basis upon which these processes operate that can lead to a potential re-allocation of family law disputes? Critics such as Shah (2014) argue that such models are, in the end, disempowering communities as they are simply constrained by liberal values, values that are 'apparently non-contestable' and do 'not problematize the potentially violent, oppressive, or absurd consequences of applying such a framework to non-liberal communities, that is, communities that do not operate from within a liberal ethical framework'.[31] Not only is the Western legal system inherently 'Eurocentric' he argues, but he challenges critiques of homogeneity, 'for seldom is homogeneity regarded as a precondition to the recognition of various types of jurisdiction, while heterogeneity does not prevent recognition in different ways'.[32] Liberal law in this reading is therefore a problem because it is based on a dominant cultural framework. This analysis should also not be taken as a claim that it is impossible for community dispute resolution mechanisms to develop alternatives to civil law mechanisms. Sharia Councils, for example, themselves are products of the Western Muslim diaspora, and not a result of a moral critique imposed from 'outside'. Observing the temporal conditions of Sharia Councils raises many issues concerning the relationship between religious identity, norms, power and politics. It is important to consider whether a parity model of gender equality could potentially allow Muslim women to be part of a process of reshaping and reconceptualizing community norms within community dispute resolution mechanisms – so how would this potentially take place and what would be the possible outcomes?

As discussed earlier, notions of choice, agency, autonomy, welfare and responsibility underpin feminist critiques of religious personal systems of law in the UK and its potential to promote equality, justice and human rights for women living within minority religious communities. This literature has been accompanied by a rise in Muslim feminist scholarship with critiques on rethinking and reinterpreting the meaning and practice of Muslim marriage, divorce and matrimonial rights upon breakdown of the relationship as part of a rethinking and reformulating of Islamic texts and intellectual thought and practice in order to 'accommodate' the needs of Muslims living in Muslim-minority contexts. With a focus on issues of sexual rights, financial obligations, honour, authority, consent and choice, this scholarship also provides important insights into the conceptual frameworks upon which issues of Muslim marriage and divorce in Islam are discussed in Muslim communities living in the 'West'. The emergence of Muslim family law in the UK must be understood as part of specific historical, social and political conditions under which postcolonial migrations emerge. Within this context feminist methodologies, ethnographic research and critiques of the 'Muslim female subject' have led to new understandings and critical approaches in the practice of Muslim family law in the UK. What is the potential of this scholarship to critically engage with Islamic feminist critiques on textual interpretations and new methodologies in re-reading sacred texts and their application to Muslim dispute resolution mechanisms?

Muslim feminist interrogation with issues of power, authority and the dynamics of power within the institutions of marriage, family, community in British Muslim communities reveals important insights into the ways in which the initiatives such as the new marriage contract and Muslim dispute resolution have been shaped, accepted, contested, resisted and challenged as part of new Muslim feminist scholarship.[33] This research also opens up important conceptual questions regarding issues of authority and power within Muslim diasporic communities and produces important insights into ways in which democratic models such as the 'Parity Democracy Model'[34] may potentially remain limited in developing ways to challenge unequal intra-community norms and values that may discriminate against its most vulnerable members, Muslim women. Furthermore the multicultural context upon which Muslim communities operate must also include critiques of democracy, dialogue and power if we are to consider the plausibility of developing positive law obligations for religious group autonomy while respecting the rights of individuals.

Parity and Sharia Councils: The Question of Gender Equality

The 'Parity Democracy Model' is an important strategic intervention in promoting equality. While recognizing the limitations of the formal substantive sex-equality framework it seeks to enable women to participate equally in all domains of citizenship. Its rationale therefore includes a transformation and redefinition of the liberal autonomy paradigm from one of independence to interdependence. In this way it resonates closely with the work of Black feminist activists and scholars, who, for example, have long recognized this paradigm shift of separated public and private spheres as individual and state law relations to intersectional analyses while recognizing the specific forms of subordination found in the family, home and community. Feminist scholarship has long addressed the fact that 'woman' is not a unitary category and instead it acts as a site of multiple contradictions with 'effects that may reinforce or undermine social divisions'.[35] We see in evidence that 'the lives of different categories of women are differentially shaped by articulating relations of power; and how under a given set of circumstances we ourselves are "situated" in these power relations vis-à-vis other categories of women and men'.[36] The challenge of universalism is addressed by creating spaces of 'strategic essentialism'[37] framed from the vantage point of a dominated subject position. Models, which therefore aspire to 'parity', are important in relation to debates on rights, democracy and law. As Rubio-Marin states,

> it seems unlikely that one could press for a gender parity democracy model in the United States without integrating some conception of racial parity democracy. This makes the project more daunting and less viable both theoretically and politically because the forces of racism and patriarchy would presumably join in opposing it.[38]

Intersectional analyses, however, raise important challenges while interrogating power relations and the defining of racial and sexual categories as oppositional and in conflict.

The question of choice, consent, agency, capabilities and autonomy has long remained both an important and a vexed question for feminist scholars from multiple traditions including Western and postcolonial feminist paradigms. The debates are underpinned by important questions of moral self and viable choices all taking place relationally under the various contexts of identity and belonging. Feminist scholarship informs us that agency cannot be exercised without choice and the relationship between choice and agency is a complex one. This relationship between agency and choice becomes even more complicated within wider debates of identity, belonging and citizenship for women living within minority Muslim communities. For many feminists, autonomy and choice remain difficult and elusive concepts to define each overlapping but also pointing to points of departure and how individual meanings and interpretations challenge the very foundations upon which they may be understood. Furthermore the acquiesce of choice is an important aspect of understanding how choice may operate.[39]

For many scholars, the question of personal autonomy and choice underpins debates on the recognition of religious councils and tribunals in Britain. The debates fall largely within two spectrums of scholarly work. The first can be described broadly as orientalist discourses which accord Muslim women little if any agency and personal choice as members of Muslim families and communities and the second points to the fact that all debates on equality and free choice are circumscribed by 'difference' along multiple and complex factors including context, place and time with notions of belonging, identity and being. The extent to which free choice is therefore expressed can simply be one based on personal and strategic decision-making in the face of conflicting and competing demands.

Thus the language of choice, commitment and faith as described by the religious scholars fits in neatly with the discourse of belonging to a wider Muslim community (*Umma*) and the importance attached to the development and formation of a local Muslim community-identity. In this way the community space (inhabited by Sharia Councils) is deemed the obvious site upon which the long-established practice of Muslim dispute resolution takes place. And in this respect it seems clear that the religious scholars seek to establish authority with respect to family law matters and require all participants to take the proceedings seriously. While the process of disputing itself reveals striking similarities to the development of family mediation in English family law, most religious scholars describe this process as distinct from the English family law approach to settling family disputes and the process is in fact framed in opposition to state law mediation practices. It is also conceptualized in terms of a *duty* upon all Muslims to abide by the requirements of the Sharia and the stipulations of the Sharia Councils. This shared understanding stems from the belief that the secular space inhabited by English family law principles cannot bring about in itself genuine resolution of matrimonial disputes for Muslims living in Britain.

In my earlier research with the exception of one interviewee, all the women had contacted a Sharia Council voluntarily, notwithstanding guidance they may have received from family, friends and/ or the local imam. In most cases, initial contact had been made via the telephone, and this was followed up with an application form citing the reasons for seeking a religious dissolution of marriage. The most obvious questions concern the autonomy and independence of the women during this process of dispute resolution and their experience of mediation and reconciliation. Although not all women are marginalized and denied equal bargaining power during official mediation processes, there exists evidence to suggest that there is deep anxiety among many women at the prospect of initiating both official and unofficial mediation, an anxiety that persists throughout the process. Feminist scholars have warned of the dangers of trying to resolve marital disputes outside the protection of formal law. This may include situations where cultural norms deny women decision-making authority or where the mediator is not neutral and yet still provides the normative framework for discussion of a situation which can transform the nature of the discussion and curtail the autonomy of the disputant. Roberts (2008) raises concerns that negotiations might well occur in private 'without the presence of partisan lawyers and without access to appeal'.[40] Some studies point to the fact that official mediation places women in a weak bargaining position, and encourages them to accept a settlement considerably inferior to one that they might have obtained had they gone through the adversarial process. Mediation can therefore promote a particular familial ideology that is based upon social control and patriarchal norms and values, and operates through subliminal, covert forms of power and coercion. In contrast, formal law provides protection against abuse in the private sphere, and so in response to the move towards private legal ordering, critics argue that mediation fails to deliver on the key issue of 'justice'. This can be described as a development of social and legal norms as one which

> exists within society a network of social norms which is formally independent of the legal system, but which is in constant interaction with it. Formal law sometimes seeks to strengthen the social norms. Sometimes it allows them to serve its purposes without the necessity of direct intervention; sometimes it tries to weaken or destroy them and sometimes it withdraws from enforcement, not in an attempt to subvert them, but because countervailing values make conflicts better resolved outside the legal arena.[41]

Feminists have extensively critiqued this tenuous relationship between family and state intervention across a wide spectrum of disciplines. Yet it is precisely the fact that women have such divergent experiences of family mediation that renders problematic any proposals to develop family mediation as a more formalized process to suit the specific needs of minority ethnic communities. There seems to be an inherent conflict between recognizing identities as multiple and fluid and formulating social policy initiatives that are based upon specific cultural practices, precisely because cultural and religious practices are open to change, contestation and interpretation. At the very least, we must ensure that mechanisms are in place so that those who choose not to participate in such processes are not compelled to do so. It is in this context that concerns have been raised about how such proposals will lead to delegating rights to communities to regulate matters of family law, which is effectively a move towards some form of cultural autonomy. Maclean rightly asks: 'What are the implications for family justice of this move towards private ordering? Is this form of "privatization" safe?'[42] Undoubtedly, in this context formal law provides protection against abuse in the 'private' sphere – the sphere in which this legal ordering operates. Maclean goes on to ask:

> is it dangerous to remove disputes from the legal system with the advantage of due process, plus protection of those at the wrong end of the far from level playing field, and visible negotiation and settlement which takes place not in court than in the shadow of the law?[43]

The debates in Ontario, Canada, have also formed the backdrop to understanding this relationship between civil and religious law. In Ontario, the extent to which family disputes should be allowed to take part under the Ontario Arbitration Act was brought into sharp relief when the Canadian Society of Muslims sought to establish a Sharia Tribunal and use the Ontario Arbitration Act to resolve family law-type disputes.

The demand for recognition of religious arbitration was made under the context of multiculturalism and underpinned by s15 of the Charter of Rights and Freedoms, a charter which guarantees fundamental freedoms including religious equality. This commitment to cultural and religious pluralism is enshrined in the Multiculturalism Act 1985 and it is this context upon which the limits of law, legality and rights are regularly debated and addressed. It is useful to evaluate the developments in Canada often referred to as the 'Ontario controversy' to consider not only the commonalities and differences between the two contexts but also questions of reform and positive law obligations.

The Arbitration Act 1991 was adopted in the Province of Ontario specifying the procedures that consenting parties could apply if they chose to resolve their disputes outside the adversarial civil law system. Of particular concern was its use among wider religious communities as traditionally the Act had been used by the Jewish Orthodox communities only to form tribunals to deal with commercial disputes and agreements (including performing religious divorces). Was this option available to all religious communities seeking to resolve matrimonial disputes? Whatever the answer to this question it became apparent that its use by Muslims communities in Canada was not only perceived as controversial but was also unforeseen. The call itself was made by a former Muslim leader and president of the Canadian Society of Muslims, Syed Mumtaz Ali, who argued that Muslims should be granted greater autonomy in matters of family law as existing provisions and constitutional arrangements failed to support the practice of their religious lives. The significance of ethnic, class and kinship differences within Muslim communities was erased to promote the view that all Muslims were religiously obligated to use Sharia to resolve family law matters. Ashe and Helie refer to this as a form of 'religio-legal pluralism' whereby religious communities are given greater autonomy in family law matters but this is only enforceable via the power of state law and civil consent orders.[44] The fact that this form of religious pluralism would not only be endorsed but be supported by the state raised alarm bells for many, notwithstanding Muslim women's organizations. And what exactly would be the role of the courts in this process? How would this type of religious governance take place? The most important and defining factor in this form of religious pluralism was the continued use of and primacy of state law. As Baines explained, 'Ali did not propose to sever the relationship between arbitration tribunals and courts. Instead he sought to restrict the role of courts to purely procedural matters: judges should not be called upon to interpret sharia law.'[45]

Under this process the courts delegated to religious authorities in matters of family law. The fact that judges were unable to intervene in potential oppressive contexts based upon orthodox religious principles was of huge concern to many Muslim women and feminists. For example, one prominent Muslim woman activist Shahnaz Khan explained,

> It is unlikely that all 'consenting' adults particularly women, would willingly and gladly consent to arrange their lives according to laws which give them unequal status before the law. Although we may characterize some women as 'choosing' no doubt they would experience a certain amount of pressure to conform. However should they decline to be governed by Muslim Personal Status Laws and find themselves ostracized by their families and their community, they would have to confront the discrimination of the larger Canadian population....[46]

Of particular concern was the unproblematized use of Sharia Law and the failure of Syed Ali and others to the potential of intra-community inequalities and injustice experienced by vulnerable women. The argument that all Muslims are obligated to use Sharia principles to resolve matrimonial disputes is also flawed and open to dispute. Opposition, therefore, came from various Muslim women's and feminist organizations including the Canadian Council of Muslim Women (CCMW) and the National Association of Women and Law (NAWL). The primary argument made was that the establishment of such tribunals led to a violation of freedoms offered to all women under existing legislation.

The Boyd Report was then commissioned in response to calls for the establishment of a civil law system to incorporate Muslim family law matters into civil law and found that religious arbitration in family law matters should be allowed to continue as long as safeguards were put into place which emphasized procedural safeguards to protect vulnerable parties who may be compelled to use these services. However, this was opposed by the largest Muslim women's organization in Canada (The Canadian Council of Muslim Women), arguing that this undermined the Canadian constitution which promotes 'equality before the law' for all its citizens. The resulting Boyd Report and critiques of Muslim women's choice in the face of moves towards religious autonomy led to the introduction of Bill 27 by Ontarian Premier McGuinty intending to ban all religious-based arbitration of family matters, marking what Ashe and Helie describe as 'Ontario's commitment to religious pluralism and its rejection of legal- and specifically religio-legal-pluralism'.[47]

Canadian Muslim women's organizations challenged this proposal and the findings of the Boyd Report which called for the recognition of religious tribunals as long as some safeguards were in place. The furore led to the government rejecting that position. As Eekelaar (2013) points out:

> The result was that, while religious bodies may still carry out arbitration in family matters under the Arbitration Act they must do so according to the law of Ontario or of another Canadian jurisdiction. Furthermore, regulations require family law arbitrators to undergo training in the law of Canada, that cases are screened for 'power imbalances and domestic violence, by someone other than the arbitrator' and that a written record be kept of the proceedings.[48]

Ayelet Shachar (2008) points out succinctly that 'The vision of privatized diversity in its fully-fledged "unregulated islands of jurisdiction" variant poses a challenge to the superiority of secular family law by its old adversary: religion.'[49] This vision of privatized diversity can be applied to the new MAT if we understand privatized diversity as a model in which to achieve and possibly separate the secular from the religious in the public space, in effect encouraging individuals to contract out of state involvement and into a traditional non-state forum when resolving family disputes. This would include religious tribunals arbitrating according to a different set of principles than those enshrined in English law.

For Shachar there are real concerns of individuals being expected to live 'as undifferentiated citizens in the public sphere, but remain free to express our distinct cultural or religious identities in the private domain of family and communal life'.[50] For her and many other liberal scholars, the issue surrounds the contentious question of where private identity and life ends and public identity begins. She quite rightly points out that, if we are expected to express personal identities in the private, at which point in the public sphere do they cease to be so? Shachar also discusses the fact that the vision of privatized diversity will evoke different feelings for different people. For those who want to establish a pluralistic system of law that recognizes claims of culture and religion, this would not be so terrifying, but those who are 'blind' to these needs will see it as challenging the superiority of universal laws that apply to all:

> for others who endorse a strict separationist approach, or 'blindness' towards religious or cultural affiliation, the idea that we might find unregulated 'religious islands of binding jurisdiction' mushrooming on the terrain of state law is seen as evidence of the dangers of accommodating diversity, potentially chipping away, however slightly as the foundational, modernist citizenship formula of 'one law for all'.[51]

In 2011 a private members bill, the Arbitration and Mediation Services (Equality) Bill, was introduced by Baroness Cox in the House of Lords. This Bill was reintroduced in October 2015 and 2016–17 and has generated considerable media attention as it aims to make clear the limits of arbitration and make amendments to the Arbitration Act to ensure its compliance with the Equality Act 2010 while seeking to outlaw discrimination on the grounds of sex. Clause 7 of the Bill proposes an amendment to the section of the Courts and Legal Services Act 1990 and criminalizes 'falsely claiming legal jurisdiction' to prevent the ousting of jurisdiction in matters of family and criminal law. Although the Bill does not specifically mention Islamic law it was widely believed to target Muslim communities and to attempt to limit the powers of organizations such as MAT and the Sharia Councils. But for many scholars it raised the question of the extent to which state law should intervene in religious councils and tribunals. It has been criticized for promoting the idea that the practice of Muslim family law is not only based upon unfair and unequal principles but specifically targets and discriminates against Muslim women as primary users of Muslim dispute resolution bodies. Furthermore the formalist top-down state interventionist approach as epitomized by the Bill in seeking to limit the powers of religious bodies has also been criticized as being predicated on fixed and homogeneous notions of Islam and Islamic legal practice which fails to recognize the dynamism and pluralism within the communities themselves. As Eekelaar (2013) argues:

> It is a mistake to think of Shari'a as a monolithic system, impervious to change. In fact the bodies apply it in different ways, and it is subject to internal arguments and contestation. Might it be better to allow it to develop within its communities and responding to its internal critiques and influenced by the culture around it? Alongside this, its adherents could be encouraged to make more use of the civil law, including a greater readiness to enter legally recognized marriages without thereby severing their relationship with their religious norms.[52]

But what are the experiences of Muslim women using religious mechanisms of dispute resolution in family law matters? Do religious tribunals promote patriarchy and gender inequality? At present, we have three significant pieces of research which provide important insights into how Sharia Councils in Britain govern as alternative dispute resolution mechanisms in the field of family law. In my work, *Shariah Councils and Muslim Women: Transcending the Boundaries of Community and Law*, I draw three key conclusions from undertaking extensive empirical research with five sharia councils and interviews with 25 British Muslim women. Firstly, the claim that seeing culture and forms of religious practice as a mode of legitimizing claims to power and authority dramatically shifts the way we understand the debate on liberalism and universalism versus relativism. In other words, the view that Muslims increasingly seek the freedom to live under sharia is not only extremely problematic but fails to capture the complexity of British Muslim identity as fragmented, porous and hybrid. Second, anthropological scholarship points to the importance of locating gender and gender relations as key sites to the debate; thus, the ways in which Muslim women engage with Sharia Councils in Britain illustrate how processes and concepts of Sharia Law are mobilized, adopted and transformed. Underlying this process are power relations that define the nature of the interaction, define meaning of sharia within Sharia Councils and construct possibilities of change and action. Finally an essentialized understanding of Muslim religious practice does not reflect the experience of British Muslim women. A more dynamic understanding of British Muslim identity is required, which does not label the needs of Muslims to accommodate sharia as fixed but understands this process as temporal, with shifts from cultural to religious practice and vice versa. Elham Manea argues that limited recognition of legal pluralism and multiculturalism has led to the recognition of culture and religion as homogeneous that ignores individual voices and arguments and the expense of collective arguments.[53] In particular her empirical research with Sharia Councils and Muslim women users of these bodies found examples of practices such as forced marriage, under-age marriage, condoning domestic violence, criminal sanctions and inequities in inheritance.

Conclusion

For many liberal scholars the practice of religious personal systems of law raises the paradox of what Shachar refers to as 'multicultural vulnerability', namely the dilemma of protecting individual choice and personal autonomy with group and community rights. The arena of family law succinctly illustrates this conflict, as Shachar explains:

> Clearly, when the state awards jurisdictional powers to the group in the family law arena, it enhances the group's autonomy. At the same time, this re-allocation of legal authority from the state to the group may also expose certain individuals within the group to systemic and sanctioned in-group rights violations.[54]

Such concerns also mirror current debates over the establishment of 'Sharia courts' in Britain and the accommodation of plural systems of family law. Some form of accommodation will include a shift of dispute resolution from the public to the private sphere and this raises serious concerns on how power is then effectively reconfigured from the state to the family and community. From such a perspective the differential treatment of women in the process of marriage and divorce can lead to a conflict between equality and autonomy and the conflicting interests of the protection of family, culture and religion as enshrined by the norms and values of Sharia Councils and the MAT.

As to the question of gender parity as a model of governance and reform it provides an important starting point for Muslim women to explore ways in which their use is based upon choice, gender equality and justice. As Anitha and Gill (2009: 168) point out:

> Women exercise their agency in complex and often contradictory ways, as they assess the options that are open to them, weigh the costs and benefits of their actions, and seek to balance their often competing needs with the expectations and desires. While there remains a need to recognise gendered power imbalances at the same time there also remains a need to respect women's exercise of agency … We need to give more support to those women who wish to express their subjectivity within the framework of the communities of which they perceive themselves to be such a fundamental part.[55]

Furthermore, the process of 'reform' within communities is often a long and fractured one, contextual and dependent upon multiple variables including state support and subsidy. Narratives from Muslim women using religious mechanisms of dispute resolution reveal both the strategic and the complex use of these bodies. In the case of Muslim legal pluralism we can then see in evidence different forms of mobilizations with underlying cultural and religious meanings which interact, conflict and re-order themselves according to the different communities in which they are located and state law, and vice versa. We see also that the decision-making processes produce an internal legal structure – a process of mixing-up, overlapping and often in conflict. The application of gender parity can also mean conflicts, meanings of equality and community recognition, or legitimacy of various legal and social domains that mix up notions of law and decision-making.

Notes

1 See Samia Bano, *Muslim Women and Shari'ah Councils: Transcending the Boundaries of Community and Law* (Palgrave MacMillan 2012); John Bowen, *On British Islam. Religion, Law and Everyday Practice in Sharia Councils* (Princeton University Press 2016).
2 See Marie Ashe and Anne Helie, 'Realities of Religico-Legalism: Religious Courts and Women's Rights in Canada, the United Kingdom and the United States' (2014) 20 *U.Cal.-Davis Journal of International Law & Policy* 139, 142.

3   Ibid 143.
4   See John Eekelaar and Maclean M (eds) *Lawyers and Mediators. The Brave New World of Services for Separated Families* (Hart Publishing 2016).
5   See Tariq Modood, 'Part One Accommodating Religions: Multicultural-ism's New Fault Line' (2013) 34(1) *Critical Social Policy* 121.
6   Lila Abu-Lughod, *Do Muslim Women Need Saving?* (Harvard University Press 2013) 6.
7   Pragna Patel, 'Faith in the State? Asian Women's Struggles for Human Rights in the UK' (2008) 16(1) *Feminist Legal Studies* 9, 25.
8   See Russell Sandberg, Gillian Douglas, Norman Doe, Sophie Gilliat-Ray and Asma Khan, 'Britain's Religious Tribunals: "Joint Governance" in Practice' (2012) 33(2) *Oxford Journal of Legal Studies* 263; Farah Ahmed, 'Personal Autonomy and the Option of Religious Law' (2010) 24(2) *International Journal of Law, Policy and the Family* 222.
9   See Modood (n 5).
10 There is a wide body of scholarship that examines the nature and prac-tice of Islamophobia. Problems on definition exist. See Salman Sayyid and AbdoolKarim Vakil (eds), *Thinking through Islamaphobia: Global Perspectives* (Hurst Press 2009).
11 See Saba Mahmood, 'Secularism, Hermeneutics, Empire: The Politics of Islamic Reformation' (2006) 18(2) *Public Culture* 323.
12 See Talal Asad, *Foundations of the Secular: Christianity, Islam, Moder-nity* (Stanford University 2003).
13 Oliver Roy, *Holy Ignorance: When Religion and Culture Part Ways* (Columbia University Press 2010).
14 See Salman Sayyid, *Recalling the Caliphate: Decolonisation and the World Order* (Hurst Press 2014).
15 Ibid 32.
16 Ibid 4.
17 See Muslim Council of Britain at www.mcb.org.uk.
18 See Muslim Women's network at www.mwnuk.co.uk.
19 See Muslim Arbitration Tribunal at www.mat.org.uk.
20 Blanca Rodriguez-Ruiz and Ruth Rubio-Marin, 'Constitutional Justifi-cation of Parity Democracy' (2009) 60 (5) *Alabama Law Review* 1171.
21 Anne Phillips, *Multiculturalism without Culture* (Princeton University Press 2007).
22 Ayelet Shachar, 'Privatizing Diversity: A Cautionary Tale from Religious Arbitration in Family Law' (2008) 9(2) *Theoretical Inquiries in Law* 573.
23 Michel Foucault, *Discipline and Punish the Birth of the Prison* (Penguin 1979) 35.
24 See Sayyid (n 14) 3.
25 See Michael Karayanni, 'The Acute Multicultural Entrapment of the Palestinian-Arab Religious Minorities in Israel and the Feeble Measures Required to Relieve It' in Robert Provost (ed), *Mapping the Legal Bound-aries of Belonging, Religion and Multiculturalism from Israel to Canada* (Oxford University Press 2014).

26 See Klaus A Ziegert, 'Systems Theory and Qualitative Socio-Legal Research' in Reza Banakar and Max Travers (eds) *Theory and Method in Socio-Legal Research* (Hart Publishing 2005).

27 See John Eekelaar, 'Law and Community Practices' in John Eekelaar and Mavis Maclean (eds) *Managing Family Justice in Diverse Societies* (Hart Publishing 2013).

28 Ibid 16.

29 See Maleiha Malik, *Minority Legal Systems in the UK: Multiculturalism, Minorities and the Law* (British Academy Policy Papers 2012) 12.

30 Ibid 65.

31 Prakash Shah, *Family, Religion and Law. Cultural Encounters in Europe* (Routledge 2014) 49.

32 Ibid 52.

33 See Ziba Mir-Hosseini, Kari Vogt, Lena Larsen and Christian Moe (eds) *Gender and Equality in Muslim Family Law: Justice and Ethics in the Islamic Legal Tradition* (I.B. Tauris 2015).

34 See Ruth Rubio-Marin, 'A New European Parity-Democracy Sex Equality Model and Why It Won't Fly in the United States' (2012) 60(1) *The American Journal of Comparative Law* 99.

35 See Avtar Brah, *Cartographies of Diaspora: Contesting Identities* (Routledge 1993) 89.

36 Ibid 93.

37 See Gayatri Spivak, 'Can the Subaltern Speak?' in Cary Nelson and Lawrence Grossberg (eds.) *Marxism and the Interpretation of Culture* (Macmillan 1988).

38 See Rubio-Marin (n 40) 105.

39 See Rosemary Hunter and Sharon Cowan (eds) *Choice and Consent: Feminist Engagements with Law and Subjectivity* (Routledge 2007).

40 See Marian Roberts, *Mediation in Family Disputes: Principles of Practice* (Ashgate 2008).

41 See Eekelaar (n 33) 45.

42 See Mavis Maclean, *Making Law for Families* (Hart Publishing 2000) 67.

43 Ibid.

44 Ashe and Helie (n 2) 151.

45 See Beverley Baines, 'Must Feminists Identify as Secular Citizens? Lessons from Ontario' in Linda C. McClain and Joanna L. Grossman (eds) *Gender Equality, Dimensions of Women's Equal Citizenship* (Cambridge University Press 2009).

46 Ashe and Helie (n 2) 152.

47 Ashe and Helie (n 2) 156.

48 Eekelaar (n 33).

49 See Shachar (n 22) 573.

50 Ibid 580.

51 Ibid.

52 Eekelaar (n 33) 32.

53 See Elham Manea, *Women and Shari'a Law: The Impact of Legal Pluralism in the UK* (I.B. Tauris 2016).

54 Shachar (n 22) 98.

55 See Sundari Anitha and Aisha Gill, 'Coercion, Consent and the Forced Marriage Debate' (2009) 17(2) *Feminist Legal Studies* 165.

Bibliography

Abbas T, *Muslim Britain: Communities under Pressure* (Zed books 2005).

Abu-Lughod L, *Do Muslim Women Need Saving?* (Harvard University Press 2013).

Ahmed F, 'Personal Autonomy and the Option of Religious Law' (2010) *International Journal of Law, Policy and the Family* 24, vol 2.

Ali S, *Modern Challenges to Islamic Law* (Cambridge University Press 2016).

Anitha S and Gill A, 'Coercion, Consent and the Forced Marriage Debate' (2009) *Feminist Legal Studies* 165, 65–184 (17) (2).

Arjana S, *Muslims in the Western Imagination* (Oxford University Press 2015).

Asad T, *Foundations of the Secular. Christianity, Islam, Modernity* (Stanford University 2003).

Asad T, 'Thinking about the Secular Body, Pain and Liberal Politics' (2011) 26(4) *Cultural* Anthropology, 657–675.

Ashe M and Helie A, *Realities of Religico-Legalism: Religious Courts and Women's Rights in Canada, the United Kingdom and the United States* (University of California, Davis 2014), vol 20.2.

Baines B, 'Must Feminists Identify as Secular Citizens? Lessons from Ontario' in Linda C. McClain and Joanna L. Grossman (eds) *Gender Equality, Dimensions of Women's Equal Citizenship* (Cambridge University Press 2009).

Bano S, *An Exploratory Study of Shariah Councils in England with Respect to Family Law* (Ministry of Justice 2012).

Bano S, *Muslim Women and Shari'ah Councils: Transcending the Boundaries of Community and Law* (Palgrave MacMillan 2012).

Booth P, 'Judging Sharia' (2008) 38 *Family Law* 935.

Bottomley A and Conaghan J, *Feminist Legal Theory and Legal Strategy* (Blackwell 1993).

Boyd S, *Challenging the Public/Private Divide: Feminism, Law and Public Policy* (Toronto University, Toronto Press 1997).

Bowen J, *On British Islam. Religion, Law and Everyday Practice in Sharia Councils* (Princeton University Press 2016).

Brah A, *Cartographies of Diaspora and Contesting Identities* (Routledge 1993).

Crenshaw K, 'Demarginalising the Intersection of Race and Sex: A Black Feminist Critique of Antidiscrimination Doctrine' (1989) *Feminist Theory and Antiracist Politics* 139, University of Chicago Legal Forum 139 (1989).

Douglas G, Gilliat-Ray S, Doe N, Sandberg R and Khan A, *Social Cohesion and Civil Law: Marriage, Divorce and Religious Courts* (Cardiff University 2011).

Foucault M, *Discipline and Punish the Birth of the Prison* (Penguin 1979).

Eekelaar J, 'Law and Community Practices' in (eds.) Eekelaar J and Maclean M (ed), Managing Family Justice in Diverse Societies (Hart 2013).

Eekelaar J and Maclean M (ed), *Managing Family Justice in Diverse Societies* (Hart 2013).

Gillat-Ray S, 'Britain's Religious Tribunals: 'Joint Governance' in Practice' (2012) *Oxford Journal of Legal* Studies 263–291 Vol 33 (No.2) Summer 2013.

Hall S, 'The West and the Rest: Discourse and Power' in Stuart Hall and Ben Gieben (eds) *Formations of Modernity* (Polity Press 1992).

Hunter R and Cowan S, 'Introduction' in Rosemary Hunter and Sharon Cowan (eds) *Choice and Consent: Feminist Engagements with Law and Subjectivity* (Routledge 2007).

Hussain Y and Bagguley S, *Citizenship, Ethnicity and Identity: British Pakistanis after the 2001 Riots* (Sage 2005).

Karayanni M, 'The Acute Multicultural Entrapment of the Palestinian-Arab Religious Minorities in Israel and the Feeble Measures Required to Relieve It' in Robert Provost (ed) *Mapping the Legal Boundaries of Belonging, Religion and Multiculturalism from Israel to Canada* (Oxford University Press 2014).

Khan S, 'Canadian Muslim Women and Shar'ia Law: A Feminist Response to 'Oh Canada!'' (1993) 6(1) *Canadian Journal of Women & Law* 52–65.

Maclean M (ed), *Making Law for Families* (Hart Publishing, (2000)

Maclean M and Eekelaar J, *Lawyers and Mediators: The Brave New World of Services for Separating Families* (Hart 2016).

Mahmood S, 'Secularism, Hermeneutics, Empire: The Politics of Islamic Reformation' (2006) 18 *Public Culture* 323–47.

Mahmood S, *Politics of Piety: Islamic Revival and the Feminist Subject.* (University of Princeton Press 2012).

Malik M, *Minority Legal Systems in the UK: Multiculturalism, Minorities and the Law* (British Academy Policy Papers 2012).

Manea E, *Women and Shari'a Law: The Impact of Legal Pluralism in the UK* (I.B. Tauris 2016).

Modood T, 'Accommodating Religions: Multiculturalism's New Fault Line' (2013) 31(3) *Critical Social Policy* 2–8.

Muslim Arbitration Tribunal, *Liberation from Forced Marriages* (2008).

Nobles R and Schiff D, *Observing Law through Systems Theory* (Hart Publishing 2014).

Patel P, 'Faith in the State? Asian Women's Struggles for Human Rights in the UK' (2008) 16(1) *Feminist Legal Studies* 9–36

Phillips A, *Multiculturalism without Culture*, (Princeton University Press 2007).

Redfern A and Hunter M, *International Commercial Arbitration* (Cambridge University Press 2004).

Roy O, *Holy Ignorance: When Religion and Culture Part Ways* (Columbia University Press 2010).

Rubio-Marin R, 'A New European Parity-Democracy Sex Equality Model and Why It Won't Fly in the United States' (2011) 60(1) *The American Journal of Comparative Law* 99.

Rodriguez Ruiz B and Rubio-Marin R, 'Constitutional Justification of Parity Democracy' (2009) 6(5) *Alabama Law Review* 1170.

Sayyid S, 'Contemporary Politics of Secularism' in Geoffrey B. Levey and Tariq Modood (eds) *Secularism, Religion and Multicultural Citizenship* (Cambridge University Press 2009).

Sayyid S, *Recalling the Caliphate: Decolonisation and the World Order* (Hurst Press 2014).

Sayyid S and Vakil AK (eds) *Thinking through Islamophobia: Global Perspectives* (Hurst Press 2009).

Shachar A, 'Privatizing Diversity: A Cautionary Tale from Religious Arbitration in Family Law' (2008) 9 *Theoretical Inquiries in Law* 573.

Shah P, Family, *Religion and Law. Cultural Encounters in Europe* (Routledge 2014).

Shah-Kazemi S, *Untying the Knot: Muslim Women, Divorce and the Shariah* (The Nuffield Foundation 2001).

Spivak G, 'Can the Subaltern Speak?' in N Nelson and L Grossberg (eds) *Marxism and the Interpretation of Culture* (Illinois University Press 1988).

Sundari A and Gill A, 'Coercion, Consent and the Forced Marriage Debate in the UK' (2009) 12 *Feminist Legal Studies* 165–84.

Index